10150389

HUMBLE KING
RETURNING KING

HUMBLE KING
RETURNING KING

Pete Kovacs

rnk RNKPublishingHouse
New York, NY 10022

Humble King Returning King
Copyright © 2006 Pete Kovacs

Requests for information should be addressed to:

RNK Publishing House LLC, MUSPB # 1000109, 445 Park Avenue, 9th Fl., New York, NY 10022, U.S.A. info@rnkpublishing.com

Library Cataloging Data

Kovacs, Pete, 1971-
    Humble King Returning King / Pete Kovacs.
    p. cm.
    Includes bibliographical references.
    ISBN: 978-0-6151-3471-0 (paperback : alk. paper)
    1. Jesus - Messiahship. 2. Jesus - Person and offices. I. Title.

Scripture quotations marked CJB are taken from the *Complete Jewish Bible*, copyright © 1998 by David H. Stern. Published by Jewish New Testament Publications, Inc. www.messianicjewish.net/jntp. Distributed by Messianic Jewish Resources. www.messianicjewish.net. All rights reserved. Used by permission.

Scripture quotations marked ESV are taken from the *Holy Bible, English Standard Version*™ Copyright © 2001 by Crossway Bibles, a division of Good News Publishers All rights reserved.

Scripture quotations marked KJV are taken from the *Holy Bible: King James Version. Public Domain.*

Scripture quotations marked NASB are taken from the *New American Standard Bible*®, Copyright © 1960, 1962, 1963, 1968, 1971, 1972, 1973, 1975, 1977, 1995 by The Lockman Foundation Used by permission." (www.Lockman.org).

Scripture quotations marked NIV are taken from the *Holy Bible: New International Version*®. NIV®. Copyright © 1973, 1978, 1984 by International Bible Society. Used by permission of Zondervan Publishing House. All rights reserved.

The "NIV" and "New International Version" trademarks are registered in the United States Patent and Trademark Office by International Bible Society. Use of either trademark requires the permission of International Bible Society.

Scripture quotations marked NLT are taken from the *Holy Bible: New Living Translation American Standard Version.* Copyright © 1996, 2004. Used by permission of Tyndale House Publishers, Inc., Carol Stream, Illinois 60188. All rights reserved.

All rights reserved. No part of this publication may be reproduced, stored in a retrieval system, or transmitted in any form or by any means, electronic, mechanical, photocopying, recording, or otherwise, without the prior permission of the publisher.

Cover design and interior layout by Pete Kovacs

Background cover image courtesy Israel Antiquities Authority

Printed in the United States of America

For Her

Contents

HUMBLE KING
RETURNING KING

Acknowledgements

You only get one first time in a lot of things, including writing a book, so here's thanks to everyone that in my mind had some part, small or great, in helping me get here.

First off, respect to my spiritual brothers in arms of P.O.D. – it's rare to find a band that at times so perfectly captured the reality of what it has meant for me to live by faith through some tough times and through new beginnings.

Although my affiliation with the Officers of the Lorne Scots (Peel, Dufferin and Halton Regiment), Royal Canadian Infantry Corps, Canadian Forces Army Reserves was cut short after I signed on because of my move to the States for work, and to begin the process of becoming a U.S. citizen, allowing me to join your regiment was my first step towards the duties and responsibilities of military service. Your nod of confidence in my potential as an infantry officer and leader will always be remembered and further honored should I be granted the privilege to serve in the near future in a new home.

To everyone at Chosen People Ministries, Mitch Glaser, Larry Rich, Justin Kron, Alan Shore, Percy Johnson, and Congregation Beth Sar Shalom, North York, ON and former Teacher Gideon Levytam, my faith was enriched during my few years of service with CPM through your understanding of Jewish culture and the Messianic Jewish perspective.

"Employ your time in improving yourself by other men's writings, so that you shall gain easily what others have labored hard for" (Socrates). Standing on the shoulders of my professors I acknowledge those professors who stood out among the rest for sharing their wisdom and learning with me whether for one semester or four years of putting up with my ideas and questions: University of Toronto at Scarborough: John Mayo (Music History), William Bowen (Music History), D.A. Bors (Psychology), A.N. Sheps (U.S. History), Modris Eksteins (European History); Tyndale University College and Seminary: John Kessler (Biblical Hebrew), Professor Emeritus Donald Leggett (Old Testament), Dennis Ngien (Theology), Professor Emeritus Erwin Penner (Biblical Greek), James Beverley (World Religions), Jeffery P. Greenman (Ethics); University of Toronto, Department and Centre for the Study of Religion: Rabbi David Novak (Jewish Studies); University of Toronto, School of Graduate Studies, Department of Near and Middle Eastern Studies: Timothy P. Harrison (Near Eastern Archaeology).

Respectful thanks to these from among my professors at Santa Clara University School of Law: Eric Wright (Torts), Allen Hammond (Contracts), Dorothy Glancy (Property), Michael Jay Jones (Legal Analysis, Research, and Writing), Ellen Kreitzberg (Criminal Law). While having to drop out from second year due to financial hardship was an unexpected turn of events, nevertheless, it was through the unending, and sometimes brutal marathon of case precedent dumped on us during 1L that I gained the unanticipated benefit of learning how to read the Biblical text with increased clarity and sense of relevance.

To everybody at the Alliance Defense Fund – Blackstone Legal Fellowship: Alan Sears, Jordan Lorence, Jeff Ventrella, Colene Lewis, and all the guest lecturers and Blackstoners of 2002, I was challenged to rethink and realign my philosophy of Law and Society more coherently with biblical foundations and emerged stronger as a result. Special thanks to Professor Steven Fitschen (National Legal Foundation/Regent University, Virginia Beach, VA) for giving me the privilege as a post-1L intern to research the fascinating case precedent of U.S. Constitutional law and for constantly reminding us interns of the importance of "the fine art of understatement," a goal I strive for whether succeeding or not.

Pastor Steve Jones, who was my pastor, mentor, and friend during the BMX Freestyle/first-girlfriend teenage years, and who encouraged me to use my spiritual gifts to God's glory, and helped put in place the values that shaped me to be the man I am today. He helped me face the reality that even through the one of the hardest times in my life, during my parents' divorce, duty and love for God meant trusting even though the pain was deeper than words can describe. His words challenged me to trust, and through trust, the peace of God kept me.

Mr. Klaus Stoeser who although he was in the humble position of being a custodian at our congregation, his depth of knowledge of the Scriptures and love for the Lord encouraged me and helped me make it through those first few turbulent years as a teenager after my parents divorced. His wisdom helped me understand how the Lord was working in my life during the times when the fire of God burned intensely within my soul.

In Israel, Captain Yonatan Goldberg (Retired) of the Israeli Defense Forces Artillery Reserves, a Northern Brigade who exemplified for me the traits of a true leader, godly husband, and father. It was during my visits to Israel that The Land and her people captured my imagination, my heart, and my soul. May God bless you, your wife, and sons with continued safety and peace in Eretz Yisrael.

To my step-dad, Paul, thank you for your generosity over the years and for allowing me to take time off work to go snowboarding at Lake Placid (February 2006) and work on the writing and research to complete the first complete version of this manuscript.

To my step-mom, Mary, thanks for taking care of my dad and bringing happiness back into his life again.

To my Mom, for always being a loving mother, and for patiently waiting for grandchildren.

To my bro, Dave, for sharing his knowledge of Math, Philosophy, and the Sciences with his little brother.

And to my Dad, who has always shown me by example what it really means to "love your neighbor as yourself" and the sacrifice this entails, would that I could be as a good a man as he.

Introduction

None of us have ever seen God with our eyes. For a believer this sometimes presents a challenge to faith simply because we're used to trusting our eyes, for the unbeliever this is the strongest reason not to believe. But even then, the strange thing is that God's existence as the infinite-personal Creator of the Universe is not at all something that seems unnatural or contradictory to our fundamental way of existing as humans, even though for most of us what it means to be human is to live life through our five senses.

Each and every day, we depend on our senses to make it through this world. As soon as we wake up in the morning and open our eyes, our brains start processing huge amounts of data just to read the time on the alarm clock and get us out of bed. We use our sense of touch to feel around and shut off the alarm and begin each new day. If you are truly blessed your sense of smell may quickly detect that life does exist in the universe because someone you love put on the coffee and its aroma fills your home. It's your sense of taste that tells you that the brown liquid in the cup that you found on the kitchen counter is, in fact, the coffee that you smelt earlier and your sense of taste also tells you that the coffee needs more sugar. We spend the rest of the day using our five senses to do whatever it is that we do. Only at the end of the day, long after the sun has set and night has come, do we close our eyes and switch into the sleep mode of human existence, which doesn't depend so heavily on the senses.

Some spiritual thinkers have associated night time with the time that our faith in God is tested, what the mystics call the dark night of the soul. But this is not the starting point in this book, although we will encounter the night of the soul later on. Our starting point is the natural place to begin for us as humans: knowing God with our senses. The foundation of our knowledge of God is not mystical experience or the experience of the transcendent in isolation from the rest of our daily life. Instead, we being at the point that God wanted us to begin, knowing his existence from the universe that he created, or what theologians call the general revelation of God. This is the most basic reason why the questions: "Does God exist, and if he does, who is he?" continues to fill the heart and mind.

To this question, God does not demand finding the answer through some kind of blind leap of faith, but instead he chose to reveal himself in the most natural way possible by entering human history, from Adam to Abraham to Messiah Jesus. In Jesus, we see a historical person, a Jewish man who lived in the 1st century C.E., revealed to our senses through history so that we can reason, argue, and debate about who he was, and is, and decide for ourselves if he really is the promised Messiah of Israel and the Light to the World. The first half of this book deals with these foundations of faith.

The second half is a collection of essays about what it means to walk by faith for those who believe, and the challenging questions that that steal faith from the soul like a thief in the night.

We will encounter the problem of evil and suffering, the night of the soul, and the nature of faith. Along the way I'll share some of my stories and experiences as I've tried to follow after Messiah Jesus, my King and my friend, a few of the virtues of godliness, and the hardship and blessings they bring.

In the spirit of friendly debate, may you be challenged in your beliefs, encouraged to remain faithful, and made strong in Messiah through these words.

To His Glory Alone.
P.A.K.
October 2006

Part I:

Foundations of Faith

Chapter One

Heavens Declare the Glory of God

"The heavens tell of the glory of God. The skies display his marvelous craftsmanship."

Psalm 19:1 [NLT]

"When you are arguing against Him, you are arguing against the very power that makes you able to argue at all."

C.S. Lewis

Chapter One

Heavens Declare the Glory of God

A large crowd of people both young and old, children and parents, singles and couples, had gathered for one purpose only, and that, to see for themselves what all the tour books and tour guides reported as the most incredible sunset you would ever see in your life; transcendent and out of the ordinary. The drive down from Athens to Cape Sounion was filled with contrasts: the deep blue sea of the Aegean, the stark white rocks of the coast of Greece, the clear sky above. Exiting the bus we looked up the hill before us to see the ancient Doric columns of the ruins of the Greek temple of Poseidon still in place after over two thousand years of human history.

We climbed our way up to the temple and found a spot amongst the ruins. The sun made its circuit down the western sky and the waves of the sea reflected its light. The mood was set for romance and "serenity now." As the sun descended closer to the sea, a warm orange glow filled the horizon and the sun lit up the waves with a beam of light as it traced its path between two mountains in the sea on either side, gradually fading below the horizon. It was no coincidence that the ancient Greeks built a temple here, for it was a sunset never to forget, and likely one of the most romantic spots on the earth, even though the marble ruins themselves were empty and cold.

The Heavens declare the glory of God

There is something about life that transcends words. Whether it is a romantic sunset overlooking the Aegean Sea or a glimpse through a kitchen window into the vastness of space and the stars in the night sky, our minds are often filled with what we describe as awe in response to the world around us. Even the most hostile atheist and convinced skeptic would not disagree that there is something about the universe that inspires the use of language such as glorious and awesome in an attempt to confine these experiences to words. The experience of wonder in response to the universe is a subjective feeling, but a subjective feeling universally shared by all of humanity.

Thousands of variations of ancient tribal and native religions based their worship on the glory seen in the skies and the earth. Some of our human ancestors worshipped the moon, others the sun and stars, others the sea and the earth, while others worshipped the animal world. Still others worshipped the image of God in humanity. In the ancient Near East, false gods were crafted from clay and stone into the form of male and female gods and goddesses. In ancient Greece, the pantheon of gods from Zeus to Aphrodite, expressed the ideal types of human achievement and ambition, love, and power. The impulse to worship as a response to the world around us is as universal in human history as it is to human experience in our contemporary world; from the historical big picture view, atheists are a minority on our planet. Where disagreements arise, they are about the nature and meaning of the subjective feelings we experience.

In order to find answers to the questions about our experience of life and the desire to worship and experience the transcendent, we must leave the cold stone and empty marble temples of the pagan world and cross the Mediterranean Sea to ascend to the Land of Israel. This is where the ancient people of God made their homes in the land that God gave to them, the Land flowing with milk and honey. This is the land of the prophets of the Lord who spoke the words given to them by the unseen God. From the perspective of the ancient Hebrew writers of the Bible, it made complete sense that the nations of the world concluded that there was a divine presence in the universe for, "the heavens tell of the glory of God. The skies display his marvelous craftsmanship" (Ps. 19:1 NLT). But because of the darkness of their minds and hearts, the nations refused to worship the creator and instead worshipped the creation (Rom. 1:21-23).

According to the Scriptures, the universe is not silent about its origin and creator, but prophetically declares the existence and character of God: "day after day [the Heavens] continue to speak" and "night after night they make him known" (Ps. 19:2-3 NLT). The revelation of God without words in creation is universally heard and "their message has gone throughout the earth, and their words to all the world" (Ps. 19:4 NLT). Religion, whether false or true, is universal to all of humanity for it derives from the very universe that surrounds us.

Whether it is atheists versus believers or skeptics versus saints, the same disagreement about how to respond to the appearance of the divine in the universe existed in the ancient world as it does today. For the ancients, it was not a conflict of belief versus doubt, but a conflict of the gods of one nation against the gods of another. For the people of God, Israel, it was the conflict of true belief in God versus idolatry. The Lord declared himself as the one true God and commanded his people Israel not to worship any other god but him (Ex. 20:3), nor to make human-made idols to worship as the nations that surrounded Israel did in their ignorance (Ex. 20:4). When God demonstrated his power to pagan kings even they understood the implication and declared to Israel that, "truly, your God is the greatest of gods, the Lord over kings" (Dan. 2:47 NLT). In the ancient world, it seems that belief in God never required any greater demonstration of power than what was seen in creation for "since the world was created, people have seen the earth and sky" and "through everything God made, they can clearly see his invisible qualities – his eternal power and divine nature" (Rom. 1:20 NLT); the heavens declare the glory of God.

The glory of God is a biblical synonym for the presence of God. The glory that is seen in the heavens is a picture of his glory. Knowing God is more than just what we experience with our senses and infinitely more complex than knowing our family or friends, but it bears a similarity.[1] What the Scriptures teach is that the wonder that we experience when we drink in the romance of a sunset overlooking the Aegean or staring up at the stars on a clear night sky or walking alone in the silence of an ancient forest is the wonder of God's existence and what it is like to be in his presence. God intended for us to begin to

---

[1] This is Dr. Packer's brilliant analogy: J.I. Packer, *Knowing God*, (London: Hodder and Stoughton, 1973), 32-35.

understand who he is simply from looking and experiencing the world around us. It is like a book we can read and enjoy or a book we choose to ignore, a book that leads us to acknowledge God as creator or to reject him. And by analogy to a book, theologians call this the general revelation of God, general because it is given to everyone, and revelation because it reveals who God is, just like the Holy Scriptures, which is the special and specific revelation of God. The heavens reveal who God is, and each day the Sun shines upon all of us as a reminder of God's existence and love for us, whether we love Him or not (Matt. 5:45).

The revelation of God in the Holy Scriptures was recorded and passed down from generation to generation, a gift from God to the world given through the people of Israel. The ancient Hebrews were soldiers, farmers, and fathers. Their understanding of who God is and why we should worship him was deeply connected to the earth, the experience of life, and the divine blessings of a passionate, faithful wife and healthy children filled with potential (Ps. 128). God created the world and humanity was uniquely created in the image of God, so that, we were made more like God himself in comparison to all other created things. Man and woman were created to know God and experience life as more than just rocks and trees, oceans and stars. We were created to experience that which transcends the material world, while at the same time resting both our feet solidly on the soil of the earth.

If there is still any doubt, life is filled with knowledge and experiences that transcend mundane, daily life. We see this in the relationship between a man and woman whose passion and deep attraction for each other leads to the mystery and beauty of sexual intimacy and the emotional bond of love (Prov. 30:19), most deeply, meaningfully, and purely experienced within the covenant relationship of marriage protected by the shield of moral goodness. It is through the passion and responsibility of marriage that human life continues through the family; functional by design and purpose, but perfectly united with the transcendent experience of love. Love may be among the greatest of human experiences and ambitions, but all of human life is filled with the transcendent. Intelligence of mind, beauty, love, strength, virtue, and other uniquely human characteristics inspire us to achieve great feats of design engineering or to create works of art that capture the divine, to strive for nobility or to make the ultimate sacrifice to defend liberty. Not only do these actions elevate those who do them, but they inspire all of humanity. It is only reasonable that our acts of nobility and the impulse to love and create derive from the Creator who made us in his own image.

Perhaps, the most remarkable of these transcendent qualities of human existence is the universality of the moral values shared across cultures and religions. Even a shallow study of the religions of the world yields the conclusion that all religions share the same ethical goals summed up in "love your neighbor as yourself" (Lev. 19:18; cf. Matt. 19:19; Rom. 13:9, etc.). Where they differ is how one actually achieves a life of moral excellence. In this regard, it is only Jesus who taught that by believing in him, we would find the way to completely wipe away the guilt and shame for our less than perfect lives, and even more, that the Lord God himself would write his laws on our hearts so that we would want to obey him and also be given the power to obey (Jer. 31:33-34; Luke 22:20; Heb. 12:24). To understand the origin of morality and see all of life and our world as the creative work of God really doesn't require a lot of faith and makes complete sense to both heart and mind. The difficulty that troubles many is that there is a competing theory to the origin of life and the explanation of its existence.

Faith and the Standard of Probability

The ancients may have fought over whose god is the most powerful, but in our contemporary world the war is fought between those who espouse faith in God as the intelligent designer and creator of our world, and those who claim that a scientific world view excludes belief in God – the faith of naturalism and evolutionary theory. God can not be put under a microscope, as the argument goes, so we can never know whether he really exists. For we can not bring God into a laboratory to be tested in the way that you or I can be tested for existence, by measuring our brain activity (even if minimal), and taking our pulse, unless of course, God chose to enter human history, and so he did.

The Scriptures do not argue with the scientist, but insist that it is by "faith we understand that the entire universe was formed by God's command, that what we now see did not come from anything that can be seen" (Heb. 11:3 NLT). Faith in God as creator does not exist in a dark room for we have the entire light of the universe that proclaims God's existence, but it still requires faith. And in requiring faith, there is an inherent mystery in the creative plan and purposes of the Lord God. He is sovereign over everything. He has the power to accomplish his will in an instant and in a manner that would cause all of us to fall on our faces and acknowledge him, but the Lord requires faith from those who desire to know him and please him (Heb. 11:6). We can argue why the Lord would require faith, but this is the reality of our human existence.

Nevertheless, while faith is required, the biblical position is that belief in God as Creator is based on observations of what actually exists in the universe, and not a blind leap from darkness into mystical light. The Scriptures encourage thorough and precise observations of what exists, i.e. good Science. Scientific data should be used to evaluate the explanations of the origin of life. It is then, in the words of evolutionary biologist and ethologist, Richard Dawkins, that we should believe the "theory of the origin of life with the least degree of improbability."[2] Thus, improbability becomes a standard to determine what is false. The importance of probability and belief was discussed by David Hume, the 18th century philosopher and historian. It was Hume who "claimed that the probability will always be greater for a natural than for a supernatural explanation of some apparently miraculous event."[3] Hume's insight is invaluable for the present discussion:

> "A wise man, therefore, proportions his belief to the evidence. In such conclusions as are founded on infallible

---

[2] Richard Dawkins, *The Blind Watchmaker: Why the Evidence of Evolution reveals a Universe without Design*, (New York: W.W. Norton & Company, 1996), 147 (cf. 41).

[3] Craig Bloomberg, *The Historical Reliability of the Gospels*, (Downers Grove, IL: Inter-Varsity Press, 1987), 77.

experience, he expects the event with the least degree of assurance, and regards his past experience as a full proof of the future existence of that event. In other cases, he considers which side is supported by the greater number of experiments: to that side he inclines, with doubt and hesitation; and when at last he fixes his judgment, the evidence exceeds not what we properly call probability. All probability, then, supposes an opposition of experiments and observations, where the one side is found to overbalance the other, and to produce a degree of evidence proportioned to the superiority."[4]

All things being equal, if improbability determines what is false, then the alleged natural explanation, evolutionary theory, should have a low degree of improbability especially in comparison to creation by Intelligent Design for it to be the true explanation for the origin of life, according to Hume and Dawkins. If evolutionary theory as an explanation depends on events that are highly improbable then it is false and should be abandoned, according to Hume and Dawkins, as an explanation of the origin of life.

---

[4] David Hume, "Enquiry Concerning Human Understanding," Section 10, Parts I-II, Miracles," in *Primary Readings in Philosophy for Understanding Theology*, ed. Diogenes Allen and Eric O. Springsted, (Louisville, Kentucky: Westminster/John Knox Press, 1992), 155.

The Argument for Intelligent Design

The natural place to begin the argument for intelligent design is not with biology, but with astronomy, for the origin of life begins first with the stars, then the earth, and then the diversity of life according to both Science and Scripture (Gen. 1). The universe itself and our place in it, on the earth, is a complex system, in the scientific literature this is known as the anthropic principle. The distance of our earth from the sun and the atmospheric makeup of our planet and other factors enable the precise conditions needed for life to exist here, so "that it appears overwhelmingly improbable that life could exist in any (imagined) universe different from this one." [5] The universe appears to have been finely tuned for our existence according to the anthropic principle, which can be summarized as follows:

"(1) the precise value of the gravitational constant, which gives us stars and planets; (2) the delicate balance between gravity, electromagnetism, and the strong nuclear force, which gives us a hydrogen-dominated universe and provides for an abundance of stellar fuel in long-lived stars; (3) the precise details of the nuclei of helium, beryllium, and carbon, which makes the production of carbon unusually efficient and thus facilitates the critical biochemistry of life; (4) the relative masses of the neutron, proton, and electron, which makes

---

[5] K. Giberson, "The Anthropic Principle," *Journal of Interdisciplinary Studies* 9 (1997), 72.

for stable long-lived atoms capable of participating in a variety of chemical reactions; and so on."[6]

Not surprisingly the anthropic principle is also found in the Scriptures in the writings of the ancient Hebrew prophet Isaiah, "He made the world to be lived in, not to be a place of empty chaos" (Is. 45:18 NLT). While evolutionary theory doesn't seek to explain the origin of the universe, but only the biological world, it depends on a world that came into existence by chance. If the universe exists by chance, its existence means that life won a lottery of highly improbable cosmic proportions. Chance as an explanation of the anthropic principle cannot be the correct answer if probability is our guide to truth. For it seems more probable that all the precise conditions needed for life to arise on the earth came about on purpose, by intent and design, even if Science cannot provide a final answer as to by whose intent and design.

Next, animal and plant life, from the household pet to obscure underwater vegetation are, as evolutionary biologist Stephen Jay Gould candidly stated, "unambiguous members of species recognized in the same way by all experienced observers. This notion of species as 'natural kinds'...fit splendidly with creationist tenets."[7] As far as what is observable with the eye, life is divided up into species just as it appears in Genesis. The Scriptures state the scientific definition of species, with each kind being able to "reproduce more of its

---

[6] Ibid. 72.

[7] Stephen Jay Gould, "A Quahog is a Quahog," *Natural History*, Vol. 88 (7), August-September, 1979, 18.

own kind" (Gen. 1:25; cf. 1:11, 12, 21, 24, 25). While this validates the biblical account of creation, it has nothing to do with probability, but there is more to the species than just consistency of reproduction.

As evolutionist Richard Dawkins stated, living organisms have "the appearance of design as if by a master watchmaker," which he insists is "the illusion of design and planning" and the byproduct of the blind watchmaker of "natural selection."[8] But Dawkins' blind watchmaker must account for all the scientific data about the species and their relationships with each other. When we observe life we see that not only do species function as individuals among the diversity of species, but certain species cannot exist without each other. This is the biological principle of mutualism, classically illustrated by the interdependent relationship between pollinizers (for example, bees and flowers), and that pollinizers are preprogrammed in their DNA to function as pollinizers; they don't learn this, they are born with this knowledge.

Certain plants, such as the genus of the Yucca plant, can only be pollinized by the Yucca moth, so evolutionary theorists conceived the concept of co-evolution – that the Yucca plant won the lottery of natural selection and the blind watchmaker produced exactly what it needed in the Yucca moth for it to survive. If the Yucca plant and Yucca moth were a freak occurrence in nature perhaps this could be easily dismissed, even though this occurring even once is highly improbable since both the Yucca plant and Yucca moth won

---

[8] Dawkins, *Blind Watchmaker*, 21.

the lottery of their existence at the same time and with exactly the conditions that they both needed to survive; it is more probable that they were designed for each other. It is all the more remarkable that mutualism occurs in thousands or perhaps even millions of interdependent relationships among species, which leads to a staggeringly high improbability if this occurred by chance evolution.

Grasping improbability is abstract so think of it like this. There is a man named Bob who lives in Smalltown, Ohio, but who can only walk two blocks because of a disability. This makes life difficult for Bob, even more so, because he can only eat hamburgers made with beef from cows raised in Texas that are fed with only Amish animal feed. Any other kind of beef and Bob will die due to an obscure hereditary condition. Even worse, all Bob has to buy Texas raised, Amish fed, beef burgers is a large box filled with Monopoly money from the 1933 edition of the game that he found by accident buried in his backyard when he was digging for oil.

But Bob is a lucky guy and in the very same town where he lives, exactly two blocks from his house, there is a hamburger restaurant owned by Lisa that imports its beef from some Amish farmers who moved to Texas from Pennsylvania by accident, their move to Texas was an accident that had no apparent reason, purpose, or explanation. Not only does this restaurant have Amish fed-Texan beef, but the only money that Lisa (the owner of the restaurant) knows exists is Monopoly money from the 1933 edition of the game. She won't accept anything else in exchange for beef burgers, and if she doesn't sell the burgers she makes, her business will go bankrupt. Both Bob and Lisa are very, very, very lucky because they both moved to Smalltown, Ohio at exactly the same time and accidentally ran into each other exactly when they moved into town.

The rest of the people in Smalltown, Ohio think that it is so weird and improbable that both Bob and Lisa would move to the same town at the same time and that Bob needs Lisa's beef burgers and that Lisa needs Bob's Monopoly money that they all believe that aliens must have dropped them into Smalltown.[9] What the residents of Smalltown, Ohio don't know is that there are thousands or even millions of other people like Bob and Lisa, but with different dietary and monetary needs. By analogy to Bob and Lisa, this is mutualism as it occurs in nature.

If probability is our standard for what to believe as truth, and what is most improbable is most likely false, then the magnitude of the improbability of species existing that depend on each other for their existence grows exponentially; this means the lotto jackpot that life won keeps getting bigger and bigger and the exact combo of numbers life needed to win keeps getting longer and longer – but there's no partial jackpot, it's either all or nothing. It is so improbable that mutualism would occur that it is far more reasonable and easier to believe that there is another simpler explanation other than chance.

---

[9] As crazy as it sounds, Francis Crick, who won the Nobel Prize in 1962 for physiology or medicine as co-discoverer of the double helix structure of DNA proposed in his 1981 book, *Life Itself,* that life was seeded on the earth by aliens.

If mutualism is the interdependence of two species, then an ecosystem is the interdependence of multiple species, which is all the more remarkable as applied to the earth as an interdependent ecosystem. Beyond mutualism between two species we find that our earth is a complex global ecosystem where minute local changes can have enormous global effects. The World Health Organization issued the following statement:

"The causal links between environmental change and human health are complex because often they are indirect, displaced in space and time, and dependent on a number of modifying forces...Deforestation may alter infectious diseases patterns, for example by affecting vector (e.g. mosquito) distributions over time."[10]

The language used by the scientists and policy makers of the WHO sounds remarkably similar to the behavior described as the "signature of chaos" of Chaos theory commonly known as the Butterfly Effect; Edward Lorenz's question, "does the flap of a butterfly's wings in Brazil set off a Tornado in Texas?"[11] Theorists consider the earth's atmosphere to be a system where chaos theory applies, but what seems to be true is that our entire global ecosystem appears to function as a dynamic

---

[10] World Health Organization, "Ecosystems and Human Well-Being: Health Synthesis," A Report of the Millennium Ecosystem Assessment, (Geneva, Switzerland: World Health Organization, 2005). Available online: http://www.millenniumassessment.org/en/index.aspx. Accessed Feb 10, 2006.

[11] Edward Lorenz quoted in Ziavddin Sardar and Iwona Adams, *Introducing Chaos*, (Duxford, Cambridge, UK: Iron Books, 1999), 26, 54.

system of complex, interdependent relationships, and one in which humanity plays an indispensable role for better or for worse. Chaos theory is said to occur in determinative, nonlinear, dynamic systems such as the earth's atmosphere. Sardar and Adams describe the butterfly effect: "Another distinguishing characteristic of chaotic systems is their sensitive dependence on initial conditions – infitesimally small changes at the start lead to bigger changes later. This behavior is described as the signature of chaos."[12] If our global ecosystem is demonstrated to be an interdependent system governed by the rules of Chaos theory, the evolution of such a system would require an astronomically high improbability deeming the occurrence of evolution highly unlikely, except on a micro level within species. If it is established with certainty that our earth functions as an interdependent ecosystem in a manner similar to our place in the universe as determined by the anthropic principle, the origin of life on our planet, by chance, becomes increasingly improbable.

The conclusion is that when evaluating evolution through the standard of probability evolution doesn't just fail to pass the test, it fails miserably. If we are to choose our theory of the origin of life according to which one, as Dawkins put it, "has the least degree of improbability"[13] then we should choose Intelligent Design. Evolution requires astronomically high improbabilities, while Intelligent Design is highly probable.

---

[12] Ibid, 26.

[13] Dawkins, *Blind Watchmaker*, 147.

For the reason that the universe, the origin of life, and the diversity of the species, appear to have been designed is because they all were actually designed, even if Science stops short of telling us who or what the Intelligent Designer was or is. This conclusion derives from Ockham's Razor, the scientific principle that can be paraphrased as: the simplest explanation is usually the correct one. Ockham's razor was the conclusion of 14th century logician William of Ockham. This principle in one form or another is one of the foundational epistemological assumptions of modern Science. If epistemology is how we know what we know, than Ockham's razor says that the simplest explanation is the correct one, and thus, the most probable explanation, which in the context of this discussion, is Intelligent Design.

The role of Science is to lead us to the most reasonable, probable, and logical explanation for the origin of life and then stop and let the theologian in every man, woman, and child make their own conclusions for what to reasonably believe about the origin of life. The great adventure of Science and scientists is to discover the unknown, like the explorers of the Renaissance, and not impose conditions upon what can or cannot be true, for that is the behavior of tyrants and dictators, not scientists. It is strange that evolutionary scientists and their followers behave as epistemological dictators depriving the school children of this generation of alternative explanations for the origin of life. Or perhaps it is not so strange. Perhaps there is something inherent in evolutionary theory that produces such behavior. Perhaps, we should not be shocked to remember that the greatest horrors of the 20th century, and arguably of all human history, and the regime that committed them were built on the foundation of Darwinian evolution and derived their theories of social Darwinism and the dehumanization and methodical extermination of those they deemed less evolved then their own highly-evolved "master race" from the Theory of Evolution.   It was the Theory of Evolution that provided the scientific and ideological justification for the atrocities that they committed. This in no way exonerates those who committed the atrocities, nor the anti-Semitic teachings and attitudes of some in the history of Christianity[14], but it is time that Darwin's ancestors, the evolutionary biologists, realize the implications of their own dogma; in the court of History the blood of millions is also charged against evolutionists and the Theory of Evolution. This cannot be ignored or forgotten. In total contrast, belief in the Intelligent Design of all humanity, made in the image of God, increases the dignity, nobility, and value of all human life: "love thy neighbor as thyself" (Lev. 19:11 KJV; c.f. Matt. 22:39).

All things being equal, Science or more accurately scientists have never claimed to offer final answers, yet evolution is offered as the final answer to the origin of life. Belief in evolution on a macro level – from amoeba to man – requires faith based on highly improbable events. The nature of

---

[14] One of the tragic facts of history is that Martin Luther who brought the Reformation to Europe through the faith of Abraham, "the just shall live by faith" (Hab. 2:4; Rom. 1:17 KJV) and seemed to be philo-semitic early in his life became hostile to the Jewish people and Judaism near the end of his life and called for the burning of synagogues, banning the preaching of Rabbis, the persecution of the Jewish people, and the destruction of Jewish literature in his 1543 treatise *Von den Juden und ihren Lügen (On the Jews and Their Lies)*. The Nazis cited Luther's treatise as justification for anti-Semitism and the Holocaust.

our world is that it appears to have been designed and this appearance of intelligent design is easily observable, but must be explained away by the evolutionist. The absence of intermediary links in the empirically verifiable fossil record falsifies the evolutionary hypothesis, but most evolutionists turn away from the obvious conclusion. Unlike evolutionary biologist and fossil-studying-paleontologist Stephen Jay Gould, who made the following observation:

"The absence of fossil evidence for intermediary stages between major transitions in organic design, indeed our inability, even in our imagination, to construct functional intermediates in many cases, has been a persistent and nagging problem for gradualist accounts of evolution."[15]

Further, after decades of trying to simulate evolution in the laboratory the only evidence that has been produced is that of evolutionary biologists' cruelty to fruit flies and not any new species. Evolution always is and always has been a theory that challenges the appearance of design in our universe not vice versa. If a scientist could exist outside of time to observe, record, and test the evolutionary hypothesis over the billions of years that it allegedly took place, perhaps some evidence would

---

[15] Stephen Jay Gould, "Is a New and General Theory of Evolution Emerging?," *Paleobiology*, Vol. 6(1), January, 1980, in *But is it Science? The Philosophical Question in the Creation/Evolution Controversy*, ed. Michael Ruse, (Amherst, New York: Prometheus Books, 1996), 187-188.

come to light. But only one being known to humanity lives outside of time, and God is on the side of Intelligent Design.

In the comparatively short existence of humanity on our planet belief in God has always been a part of life. The Scriptures teach that this is so because he designed the world to reveal his existence. God does not force us to acknowledge that he is the creator and that the heavens display his glory. He desires worshippers who worship him in spirit and in truth. The Lord rejoices when he examines our hearts and "finds integrity there" (1 Chron. 29:17 NLT), and all of heaven rejoices when one sinner "returns to God" (Luke 15:7 NLT). It is our choice. We can live in the empty marble temples of the ancient world and the cold stone temples of godless scientific institutions or we can receive the revelation through creation of God's existence and glory and say like the great King David of Israel, "one thing have I asked of the Lord, and that will I seek after: that I may dwell in the house of the LORD all the days of my life, to gaze upon the beauty of the LORD and to inquire in his temple" (Ps. 27:4 ESV). The heavens declare the glory of God, but then, if so, how can we know who he is? The path to the house of the Lord begins at the feet of Jesus.

Main thought:
: The glory that we see in the heavens is what it is like to be in the presence of God and declares his existence; faith is always required to please God, but faith is built on the foundation of reason.

Key Verse:
: *"The heavens tell of the glory of God. The skies display his marvelous craftsmanship."* Psalm 19:1 [NLT]

Question:
: Why do we experience the sense of transcendent wonder and awe as a response to the universe if not because God purposefully created the world to testify and reveal his transcendent existence just as the Scriptures claim?

Chapter Two

Jesus was Jewish

"The people of Israel! They were made God's children, the Sh'kinah has been with them, the covenants are theirs, likewise the giving of the Torah, the Temple service and the promises; the Patriarchs are theirs; and from them, as far as his physical descent is concerned, came the Messiah, who is over all. Praised by Adonai for ever! Amen."

Romans 9:4-5 [CJB]

"Rabbi, you want Moshiach? You got Him! Yeshua Ha'Mashiach a.k.a. Jesus Christ. There you go. Your prayers have been answered. Mazel Tov! Let's eat!!!!"

Aviad Cohen (50 Shekel)

Chapter Two

Jesus was Jewish

Jesus was Jewish. Even a quick read through the New Testament Gospels will leave no doubt in the reader's mind. Not only was Jesus born into the mishpocha (family) and community of Judaism in the first century C.E., but Jesus' jewishness was central to his identity and purpose. For something so obvious and so fundamental to who Jesus was, it defies human understanding that Jesus' jewishness was largely ignored for most of the history of Christianity. In more recent times there has been an awakening of interest in Jesus and his jewishness. But alongside this awakening some Christian scholars have taken the traditional apathy to Jesus' jewishness in the Christian church to the next level to the point of challenging his very historical existence. To be sure doubts about whether Jesus existed as a historical figure are usually found among liberal, Christian scholars who continue their never-ending quest for the historical Jesus with the never-ending result that they can't find him. In contrast, Jewish scholars take ownership over Jesus as one of their own, "but that Jesus was a Jew, a son of the Synagogue, is beyond doubt."[1]

---

[1] Samuel Sandmel, *Judaism and Christian Beginnings*, (New York: Oxford University Press, 1978), 398.

The apathy or outright hostility to the jewishness of Jesus and the Jewish roots of the Christian faith has its origins in the early church fathers. Arguably, the roots of this apathy trace to the Hellenistic or Platonic philosophy of church fathers like Origen, whose emphasis on the non-material and non-temporal found less significance in the physical-historical Jewish context of Jesus as Messiah of Israel. This was already a departure from the biblical-Hebraic worldview, which was deeply connected to the worship of the Lord in the Temple in Jerusalem, the relationship between the religious life cycle and agricultural seasons, and the acts of the Lord's redemption and miracles throughout the history of Israel. In 325, the First Council of Nicea decided to officially separate the commemoration of the crucifixion and resurrection of Jesus from the Jewish festival of Passover motivated by anti-Semitism and hostility towards Judaism. Emperor Constantine who had officially converted to Christianity and convened the Council wanted to insure that Christian Passover or Easter be removed from any connection to the Jewish people and biblical Passover.

From this point on up until the late 19th and 20th centuries, the Christian church by and large did not concern itself with Jesus' jewishness or the Jewish roots of the Christian faith. In the 20th century, the Messianic movement came into being as Jewish men and women raised within Judaism became believers in Jesus. This along with the establishment of the State of Israel in 1948 and the return of Jerusalem to Jewish rule in 1967 is commonly held to be related to this Jewish re-birth within Christianity and the beginning of the end of what is called in the New Testament "the time of the Gentiles"; *"Jerusalem will be trampled on by the Gentiles until the times of the Gentiles are fulfilled"* [Luke 21:24 NIV].

The primary source for knowing who Jesus was are the New Testament Gospels and letters, but any doubt to the historical existence of Jesus is ruled out simply because of the abundance of ancient sources outside the New Testament that refer to him, 45 ancient sources by one scholars count yielding 129 specific facts about the "life, person, teaching, death, and resurrection of Jesus."[2] The point cannot be overlooked that ancient history is "based on many fewer sources that are much later than the events that they record,"[3] which makes sense since Jesus' importance in history was pivotal and unparalleled: Jesus is the most famous Hebrew who ever lived.

Jesus as Jewish in the Gospels

The first four books of the New Testament, Matthew, Mark, Luke, and John, are called the Gospels. All the writers of the Gospels had a close connection to Judaism. Matthew was Jewish, descended from the tribe of Levi. Mark was Jewish. Luke was a doctor and a gentile convert to Judaism. John was Jewish, a friend of the High Priest (John 18:15), and wrote his Gospel last among the four. He, along with Peter and James,

---

[2] See Gary Habermas, *The Historical Jesus: Ancient Evidence for the Life of Christ*, (Joplin, Missouri: College Press, 1996), 250.

[3] Ibid., 251.

were the inner circle of Jesus' disciples. Not surprisingly they all include specific details of Jesus' jewishness.

As far as his physical descent, Jesus was born into a Jewish family and Jewish religious context in ancient Israel. Today, he would be called a Sabra.[4] While there is debate about who can rightly be considered Jewish, the strictest rabbinic definition is someone who has a Jewish mother. Believers and skeptics may disagree about who the father of Jesus was, but no one doubts that his mother was Mary, or in Hebrew Miryam. She was a virgin, a pure Jewish young woman whose beauty flowed from her love for God and who glorified the Lord for his fulfillment of his promises to her "ancestors, to Abraham and his children forever" (Luke 1:55 NLT). All things being equal, the Christmas story of the birth of Messiah in Bethlehem is the story of a beautiful, young Jewish woman giving birth to her son (Matt. 1:18-2:1; cf. Luke 2:1-6).

Jesus lived life through the Jewish Life Cycle

Jesus participated in the unique, cultural observances that are known as the Jewish life cycle. By the will of his Jewish parents, Jesus was circumcised (Brit Milah) on the eighth day at the Temple (Luke 2:21). He was raised in a Jewish home and celebrated Jewish holidays with his family (Luke 2:41), which in his time often meant making the trip up

---

[4] Sabra means native born Jewish-Israeli.

to Jerusalem from his home in Nazareth to keep the holy days at the Temple. Jesus attended Jewish weddings, even miraculously creating wine out of water at the wedding in Cana (John 2:1-11); a sermon without words of his divinity as the creator of the fruit of the vine (recall the Jewish blessing over wine: '*Baruch Atah Adonai Elohaynu Melech Ha'olam boray pri hagafen*' – Blessed are you Lord our God, King of the Universe, Creator of fruit of the vine.). As Jesus said at a later time, "Just believe that I am in the Father and the Father is in me. Or at least believe because of the work you have seen me do" (John 14:11 NLT).

Later in adult life Jesus observed the Shabbat and went to synagogue each Sabbath morning where we know he read from the Hebrew scrolls and taught in his own and other synagogues in ancient Israel (Matt. 9:35, 12:9, 13:54; Mark 1:21, 1:39, 3:1, 6:2; Luke 4:15-16, 4:31, 4:44, 6:6, 13:10; John 6:59). He was often invited over as a dinner guest to the home of Jewish religious leaders (Luke 7:36, 14:1), which very likely happened on Erev Shabbat (Friday night) since this is when it is custom for Jewish families to celebrate the beginning of the Sabbath and enjoy a good meal with family and guests (but this is speculation and not clearly indicated in the Gospel texts). The Sabbath was important to Jesus.

In a difficult passage in the Gospels, Jesus called himself the "Lord of the Sabbath" (Matt. 12:8; Mark 2:28; Luke 6:5) in response to the rebuke of some rabbis of the Pharisaic sect who thought he should have reprimanded his disciples for failing to properly observe the Sabbath. This was a direct challenge to Jesus' allegiance to and observance of the Law of Moses. Jesus' response must be interpreted in the light of what the Sabbath means within Judaism. Tradition in Judaism teaches that the Sabbath is a celebration of the future eternal life with God: "Israel: 'But even in the world should we have a foretaste of that other?' God: The Sabbath will give you this foretaste.'"[5] Or as one Rabbi wrote, "keeping the Sabbath *is* living in God's kingdom [original emphasis]."[6] When Jesus called himself "Lord of the Sabbath" he wasn't just asserting his rightful authority as Messiah over the Law, he was saying that he was the divine source of the Law and the King of the eternal Kingdom of God that was celebrated on the Sabbath; Jesus was saying that he was both Messiah and the divine Son of God in language that only his Jewish brothers would understand. The rabbinic challenge against his allegiance to the Law only made sense because of the fact that Jesus kept, taught, and highly valued the Law of Moses and encouraged others to do so (Matt. 5:17-20, 8:4; Mark 1:44, 10:3, 10:19, 12:26; Luke 5:14, 18:19; John 5:45-46). As Jesus said, "not even the smallest detail of God's law will disappear until its purpose is achieved" (Matt. 5:18 NLT).

Jesus also kept the Jewish holidays. He celebrated Passover with his family as a boy every year (Luke 2:41).[7]

---

[5] Quoted in Mark Zborowski and Elizabeth Herzog, *Life is with People: The Jewish Little-Town of Eastern Europe*, (New York: International University Press, 1952), 37.

[6] Jacob Neusner, *The Way of Torah: An Introduction to Judaism*, second edition, (Encino, California: Dickenson Publishing Company, 1974), 37.

[7] This is the story of Jesus debating with the religious leaders in the Temple. This cannot be Jesus' bar mitzvah as some have suggested because Luke clearly says that Jesus was twelve years old (Luke 2:42) and had not yet reached the age of Bar Mitzvah (thirteen years plus one day). Further, this event certainly didn't happen on the Sabbath (Jesus' Bar Mitzvah would have taken place on the first Sabbath after he turned 13) because Jesus and

Later as an adult he celebrated the Passover Seder with his disciples as well as the Feast of Unleavened Bread (Matt. 26:17-30; Mark 14:12-26; Luke 22:14-20; John 2:13). We also know that Jesus kept Succoth and traveled up to Jerusalem to observe this holiday (John 7:2-10), he observed another unspecified Jewish festival (John 5:1), and also celebrated Chanukah, the Festival of Lights, in Jerusalem (John 10:22-23). Notably absent from the New Testament Gospels is any observance of Yom Kippur, the Day of Atonement, which is considered the holiest day in the religious calendar in Judaism. This is surely by intent since Jesus taught that only through believing in him as Messiah and his atoning sacrifice (John 3:16-18) could ones name be inscribed in the Book of Life (see Revelation 20:11-15 for John's vision of the future and final Yom Kippur).

The period of Jewish history that Jesus lived in is known as the Second Temple Period (520 B.C.E. to 70 C.E.). While worshipping at the Temple is not possible for observant Jews today since there is no Temple, during the first century it was the physical and spiritual center of Judaism; it is for this reason that the Kotel – the Western Wall – is the holiest site in Judaism today. Jesus regularly went to the Temple and was zealous that worship be conducted there according to the Law (Mark 11:15-25, 13:1; Luke 19:45-48, 21:1; John 2:13-20). The Gospels give a glimpse into Jewish worship during the Temple period and report that Jesus taught in the courts of the

---

his family traveled back to Nazareth on the same day. They wouldn't have traveled back if it was the Sabbath.

Temple during Succoth (John 7:14, 28) as well as during Chanukah (John 10:23).

Jesus' Jewish identity was not just personal, but also embodied his primary purpose as the Shepherd of Israel – the promised Messiah – to "help God's lost sheep – the people of Israel" (Matt. 15:24 NLT). This was not motivated out of a belief that the Gentiles were not worthy of his attention, but because Messiah was promised to Israel. Although, we know that Jesus healed, taught, and accepted followers among the Gentiles during his lifetime (Matt. 15:28; Luke 7:10; John 4:1-42), the focus of his love was for his own people and family, Israel. He said he was the Messiah – the Messiah of Israel (Matt. 26:62-64; Luke 7:19-23, 18:31, 22:66-71, 23:3, 24:25-27, 24:46; John 1:49-51, 4:26, 11:25-26, 13:19). This being the case surprisingly he warned his disciples not to tell anyone else that he was the Messiah (Matt. 16:20), for in God's plan his own people had to reject him, even though many religious and non-observant Jews believed that he was the Messiah during his lifetime (Matt. 1:16; 16:16, 27:17; Mark 8:29; Luke 2:25-35, 9:20; John 1:41, 2:23, 4:42, 7:31, 11:27, 12:12-15), including secret-believers, like Rabbi Nicodemus (John 3:1,4,9, 7:50, 19:39), and religious leaders, like Joseph of Arimathea, a member of the Sanhedrin (Matt.27:57; Mark 15:43; Luke 23:50-52; John 19:38); "Every teacher of religious law who becomes a disciple in the Kingdom of Heaven is like a home-owner who brings from his storeroom new gems of truth as well as old" (Matt. 13:52 NLT).

After his resurrection belief in Messiah Jesus spread throughout the world-wide Jewish community and into the gentile world fulfilling Isaiah's prophecy that Messiah would be a "light for the Nations" (Isaiah 42:6). In this regard, Messiah was the personification of Israel's role to be a light for the Nations. No other Jewish man in human history who also claimed to be the Mashiach has been believed to be Messiah among the Gentiles. Belief in Jesus as the promised Messiah of Israel which began in 1st century Israel has spread to nations all around the globe over the last 2000 years and will come near full circle as it reaches the Muslim world. Jesus said that the "gospel of the kingdom will be preached in the whole world as a testimony to all nations, and then the end will come" (Matt. 24:14 NIV), and then Jesus will return to Israel as Mashiach Ben-David (Rom. 11:25-27).

Messiah: The Big-Picture Historical Background [8]

Jesus was Jewish, but his place as the promised Messiah of Israel only makes sense in the context of the fulfillment of the bigger picture: God's historical covenants with Israel. There are six covenants God made with humanity. The covenants are contracts between God and man and the terms of these covenants include the blessings, curses, and promises of God.

Two covenants were made before God chose Israel as a people for himself. The first is the Adamic covenant God made with Adam after Adam and Eve sinned and were thrown out of

---

[8] This section was influenced by Walter C. Kaiser, Jr., *Toward an Old Testament Theology*, (Grand Rapids, Michigan: Zondervan, 1978).

the Garden of Eden (Gen. 2:15-17; 3:9-24). Because they violated God's commands, evil, suffering, and conflict became the reality of human existence.[9] The second covenant was made with Noah, the Noahic covenant, after the flood waters receded. This covenant was made legal and binding through blood when Noah sacrificed animals and birds to the Lord and the Lord promised that he would never again destroy living things on the earth, including humanity "even though everything they think or imagine is bent toward evil from childhood" (Gen. 8:21 NLT). God accepted Noah's sacrifice and gave the Noachide laws which were to be observed by all nations and peoples (Acts 15:23-28).

Abraham is considered to be the father of three faiths, Judaism, Christianity, and Islam, and with Abraham God made his third covenant, the Abrahamic covenant. God's covenant with Abraham began with his call to go to "the land I will show you" – the land of Israel (Gen. 12:1 NLT). This covenant included God's promise to bless Abraham and his people, and to curse "those who treat you with contempt" (Gen. 12:3 NLT). It was made legal and binding upon God himself through blood when Abraham sacrificed animals to God (Gen. 15:9-11). This covenant included the promise that Abraham's descendants would be numerous, but would suffer for a time in Egypt. The outward sign of this covenant was circumcision, legally-binding on each Jewish male by their own blood (Gen. 17:10-12; Ex. 4:25-26). The first sign of God fulfilling his promise to Abraham was the birth of his son Isaac, through whom God's

---

[9] Some argue that even this covenant required animal sacrifice because God killed animals to make clothing for Adam and Eve (Gen. 3:21).

blessing would continue. This covenant promised that through the people of Israel "all the families on earth" would be blessed (Gen. 12:3 NLT).

The next covenant God made was with Moses and the People of Israel at Sinai (Ex. 19–24). This was the giving of the divine law and the promise of God's blessings and cursing for obedience and disobedience. After Moses instructed that burnt offerings and animal sacrifices be made to the Lord (Ex. 24:5) Israel accepted the terms of this covenant and promised that they would do everything written in the law (Ex. 24:7). In response, Moses sprinkled the people of Israel with the blood of the sacrificial animals making the terms of this covenant binding upon Israel. While animal sacrifice seems brutal and gory to the contemporary reader it was crucial to God's covenants. The Mosaic covenant introduced regular animal sacrifice in the Tent of Meeting, which later continued in the Temple (Beth HaMikdash) in Jerusalem. In God's justice and mercy he knew that Israel could not keep his law perfectly, so he provided a way to receive forgiveness through animal sacrifice and the shedding of blood for the atonement of sins (Lev. 17:11). The blood of the Passover lamb was what saved Israel from Egypt on the night of Passover and on Yom Kippur it was blood that atoned for sins (Lev. 16:10).

The next covenant was the Davidic covenant (2 Sam. 7). With Abraham, God had chosen Israel as the nation that he would bless and cause to be a blessing to all of humanity. With Moses, God had given his law to teach Israel what pleases God and what displeases him (i.e. sin), and provided the way to be forgiven for sin through the blood of sacrifice. With David, God's covenant took on a kingly perspective. God's promise to

David was that he would make him the beginning of a kingly dynasty of rulers who would strengthen Israel as a nation state, and that his son, Solomon, would build a temple for God's glory, where God himself would be present – the Sh'kinah. God's promise to David was that his dynasty of rulers and his kingdom would continue "for all time" and that his throne would "be secure forever" (2 Sam. 7:16 NLT). This is the covenant promise that placed the hope of God's deliverance of Israel in the Messiah – the Anointed King who would rule on David's throne forever like no other human kingdom or earthly ruler.

It is with God's final covenant that Jesus' Jewish identity within the context of the covenants of Israel finds its place. This final covenant is called the New Covenant (in Hebrew: 'HaBrit HaChadashah'), also known as the New Testament. It is found prophesied in the book of the Hebrew prophet Jeremiah (Jer. 31:31-37). This covenant like previous covenants was for "the people of Israel and Judah" (Jer. 31:31 NLT). The significance of this covenant is that it did not add terms of contract that could be broken or disobeyed like the one the Lord made with Israel through Moses, that in God's eyes, Israel failed to keep (Jer. 31:32). Through the terms of this covenant God himself would make sure that his people would obey his laws because he promised to "put my instructions deep within them" and "write them on their hearts" (Jer. 31:33 NLT). God promised that he would change the evil nature of their hearts that had displeased him since the days of Noah (Gen. 8:21) and give a desire to obey him and the power to obey. God promised he would "forgive their wickedness" and "their sins" (Jer. 31:34 NLT) and that just as sure as the

Lord held together the laws of the universe, he would never reject his people Israel for their sins (Jer. 31:35-37). This is the prophecy concerning God's New Covenant with Israel.

The fulfillment of Jeremiah's words took place in the year 30 C.E. during Passover in Jerusalem. Jesus had asked his disciples to prepare a place for them to celebrate the Seder (Passover dinner) together (Matt. 26:26-29; Mark 14:22-25; Luke 22:19-20; 1 Cor. 11:23-26). They found a place in the upstairs room of a house in Jerusalem. They ate the meal in remembrance of God's deliverance of Israel from Egypt and the blood of the Passover lamb that saved them when the Lord killed the firstborn sons of the Egyptians because of Pharaoh's refusal to set the children of Israel free from slavery. During the Passover meal Jesus took another cup of wine and infused it with the meaning of redemption: "This cup is the new covenant between God and his people – an agreement confirmed with my blood, which is poured out as a sacrifice," (Luke 22:20 NLT). Like the covenant with Moses and Israel this covenant was made legal and binding through blood sacrifice, but it was to be the blood sacrifice of the promised Messiah himself in fulfillment of the prophecies of the Hebrew prophet Isaiah who foretold the suffering servant of the Lord would be "pierced for our rebellion" and "crushed for our sins" (Is. 53:5 NLT; cf. Heb. 8:1–10:18). God's new covenant with the people of Israel was made legally binding and in effect with the suffering and death of Jesus, whom the Romans scorned as the King of the Jews, but who rose from the dead as the King of Israel.

The modern Passover Seder has four cups of wine. Of the four, the third cup is the "Cup of Redemption," which many believe is the cup that Jesus referred to in the Gospel accounts. But it is not clear when historically the Seder took on its current form. There are remarkable analogies to Messiah Jesus in the current form of the Seder. Some of these are, first, the Cup of Redemption, which symbolized the redemption of Israel through the blood of the Passover Lamb, Jesus explained was a symbol of the redemption through his blood – Messiah Jesus is called "our Passover Lamb" in 1 Cor. 5:7. Second, the three pieces of matzah in the Matzah Tosh possibly representing the Trinity: Father, Son, and Holy Spirit – Rabbis explain represent Abraham, Isaac, and Jacob or the Cohenim, the Leviim, and Am Yisrael, but no one knows for certain from where this tradition originates. Third, the second piece of matzah in the Matzah Tosh representing the Son – Messiah Jesus – that is "broken" represents the beating and crucifixion of Jesus. Fourth, the matzah that is "striped" like Jesus was from being beaten a.k.a. Isaiah 53:5 (KJV) and "pierced" as Messiah was at the crucifixion. Fifth, the Afikomen, which is broken off from the second piece of matzah, like Jesus was broken for our sins at the crucifixion, is hidden and is then found by the children after the meal as a symbol of the resurrection of Messiah. Sixth, the literal translation of "afikomen" appears to be "the coming one" or "one that comes after" (i.e. returns), which is an uncanny fit with the resurrection symbolism in the Seder, and also a reference to the Second Coming/Return of Messiah.

The current form of the Seder may have been codified during the Graeco-Roman period due to the custom of reclining while eating as was common during the Roman period and the reference to reclining found in the Seder Haggadah, and the presence of the Greek word "afikomen," which is the only Greek word in the traditional Seder Haggadah. For these reasons some have suggested that because of the remarkable fit of symbolism with Messiah Jesus and the story of his redemption the current form of the Seder as practiced in Judaism today may actually represent Nazarene (Jewish-Christian) beliefs from the 1st or 2nd century C.E.; this is obviously controversial.

The Resurrection and a Rabbi

There can be no doubt that Jesus lived a Jewish life and his death makes no sense apart from his jewishness as the fulfillment of the historical covenants that God made with Israel. But God's covenants would have failed if the story ended with Jesus' death. Jesus was the son of David, the promised Messianic King who would rule on the throne of David forever (Rev. 22:16; Rom 1:3). The resurrection was and is central to belief in Jesus as Messiah for if Messiah did not rise from the dead then believing in him is "useless" and there could be no atonement for sins (1 Cor. 15:15 NLT). No Jewish person waiting for the Messiah – the Son of David – to rule and reign on the Throne of David would have believed in a dead Messiah. Thus, the followers of Jesus were accused right from the beginning of making up stories about Jesus and the resurrection. They responded to these accusations during their lifetime. They stated that they were "not making up clever stories" about Jesus (2 Pet. 1:16 NLT) and that they were not "lying" (1 Cor. 15:15 NLT), but that the resurrection was a "fact" (1 Cor. 15:20 NLT), and that 500 people together had seen Jesus alive after he had been executed, and these people were still alive when the New Testament was being written (1 Cor. 15:6), so that those who read the testimony of these witnesses could have easily confirmed or negated what was written.

The leaders among the first Jewish believers in Jesus during the 1st century (i.e. the Apostles) were public figures. A public figure is "a person who has achieved fame or notoriety or who has voluntarily become involved in a public controversy."[10] In our day, they have access to the media (newspapers, television, etc) to make statements that are widely heard by a large audience. In the first century, the New Testament letters were the form of media the Apostles used to communicate their message. Just as in our day, when a public figure, say for example a president, makes a statement that is false or his audience suspects is a lie, almost as if by natural law, his lie is quickly found out. Today, this happens literally at the speed of light through the media, but in the first century it would have taken longer – but certainly not a whole century. As time increases after a public figure has made a statement so the number of people increase who will hear the statement, and try to find out if it is true. As long as the facts are still accessible, this increases the likelihood that a false statement will be exposed as a lie; the larger number of people that hear a statement, the more likely that it will be proven true or false

---

[10] This is a legal category assigned to a person when deciding a defamation claim in tort law. Defamation occurs when a person's reputation is harmed by a "false statement to a third person." *Black's Law Dictionary*, 7th ed., s.v. "Defamation."

with certainty. This is why the Apostles responded to the defamation made against them through the New Testament letters, so their words could be tested by the public, and why they stated explicitly that they were not lying; it is just like a public figure responding to an accusation against them through the Washington Post. The Apostles' response, which was essentially "ask the five hundred eyewitnesses if we're lying," gave the public the objective means to verify the statements about the resurrection, and placed the burden of proof[11] back on those who accused the Apostles of lying; their accusers had to prove that their defamatory statement, "The Apostles are lying," was true, and that the testimonies of the witnesses to the resurrection were false.

It is significant, that historically we do not know of any evidence that was brought forward to prove that what the Apostles said was a lie. This all happened while those who were witnesses to the resurrection were still alive. The New Testament book of First Corinthians, where Paul makes the claim that 500 people saw Jesus alive, was written around 57 C.E., placing it only 27 years after the resurrection itself; these same people would most likely have known Jesus before and after his death and resurrection. The crucified, dead corpse of Jesus was never brought forward, which would have instantly falsified the claims of the resurrection; even those who knew him, but didn't believe would have easily been able to identify

---

[11] "Burden of Proof" is a legal term. The person who has to show enough evidence to prove that what they say is true (Burden of Production), and convince others that what they say is true (Burden of Persuasion) is the one who carries the burden of proof. *Black's Law Dictionary*, 7th ed., s.v. "Burden of Proof."

the body. Nor were the testimonies of the hundreds who saw Jesus alive shown to be false. Where is this historical evidence that the Apostles were lying? Why did any anyone believe their claims? If the New Testament writers were lying they would have been exposed as frauds 2000 years ago, but not only were they not exposed as liars, but thousands living in Israel and the ancient Mediterranean region believed that Jesus was the Messiah, both Jews and Gentiles (Acts 2:41, 4:3-5, 5:14, 9:42, 11:21, 13:12, 14:1, 16:34, 17:12, 18:8, 21:20).

Traveling back in time, think of it like this. One Shabbat, a rabbi hears Rabbi Shaul (Apostle Paul) preaching in his synagogue about the resurrection. He is skeptical and finds the claim unbelievable, but since the rabbi is a righteous man, and personally knew Rabbi Gamaliel (Paul's teacher) – the reason he invited him in the first place, he gives Shaul the benefit of the doubt and speaks with him after the service to get a few names of the people among the 500 that all saw Jesus at the same time after he rose from the dead. Over the next few weeks, the rabbi visits these people and asks them to tell their stories. Since a rabbi knows people well and is gifted with wisdom from God and studies Torah, both written and oral tradition (i.e. studies Law just like judges and lawyers do today[12]), he can tell the difference between truth and lies,

---

[12] The Torah (Five Books of Moses/Pentateuch) is analogous to statute law/law codes, while the oral tradition, as later recorded in the Talmud, is analogous to case precedent and embodies rabbinic interpretations of the law. The disputes between Jesus and the Pharisees over the Law, as found in the New Testament, are pre-Talmudic evidence of this oral tradition. What is often falsely portrayed as Messiah's rejection of the Law of Moses was, in fact, his rejection of specific Pharisaic interpretations of the Law.

between someone who is telling the truth and a liar. Each story he hears makes sense, and even when he tests them by asking them to repeat a fact they said a few minutes earlier to see if they change their story, they don't change their story (think of what customs officials do when we cross the border, or when a witness is cross-examined during trial).

After a few weeks, the rabbi still isn't a believer, but he tells his congregation, and other local rabbis, that he spoke with those who claim to have seen Jesus alive after the crucifixion, and he doesn't think their stories are false. He adds that he's still not convinced that Jesus is the Messiah since he didn't establish the messianic kingdom and liberate Israel from Roman occupation. Over time people stop accusing the Apostles of lying because so many rabbis and others have evaluated the stories and found them to be true. Some among the rabbi's congregation begin to believe that Jesus is the Messiah; even some of the rabbi's own family. Over time, the rabbi becomes a believer, but in secret. Only one other rabbi in his area is a believer like him, and although the other rabbis know, they don't say anything.

Now multiply that times every rabbi, religious leader, and congregation in the tight knit community of Israel in the 1st century where everyone had relatives all over the country,

---

Even within the Talmud there are varying interpretations of the Mosaic Law, which teaches judgment and discretion. This is analogous to law schools today where law students study case precedent to learn the law (i.e. Brown v. Jones). Case precedent records how judges have interpreted the law through specific conflicts brought to trial for resolution and it is these judicial opinions that law students read and discuss. Through this process they also learn how to think with the sense of relevance and discretion needed to be lawyers, and for some among them, future judges.

and you have the test of truth that the Apostles had to pass; Israel, then and now, wasn't just a nation, but a family. The significance of this is that 1st century Israel and the Jewish communities scattered around the Mediterranean, under the leadership of an army of judges and lawyers (Cohenim, Levites, Rabbis, religious scribes, etc.), would have been less gullible and less likely to believe stories of a miraculous resurrection of the Messiah. Remember that the first believers were all themselves members of this same community where the resurrection and growth of belief in Jesus as the Messiah began. They were all either Jewish by birth or converts to Judaism.

There really is no simpler and more logical explanation for the belief in the resurrection of Jesus and the explosion of belief in Jesus as Messiah that began in Jerusalem soon after 30 C.E. than that Jesus truly did rise from the dead in human history. We see the effect today as millions of people, Jews and Gentiles, around the world continue to believe in him as Messiah; this demands a historical cause. By defeating death Messiah Jesus arose to rule on the throne of David forever, and the implication can't be missed, not only was Jesus Jewish, but he still is.

Main Thought: Jesus was Jewish and he still is.

Key Verses: "The people of Israel! They were made
                  God's children, the Sh'kinah has been
                  with them, the covenants are theirs,
                  likewise the giving of the Torah, the
                  Temple service and the promises; the
                  Patriarchs are theirs; and from them, as
                  far as his physical descent is concerned,
                  came the Messiah, who is over all.
                  Praised by Adonai for ever! Amen."
                  (Romans 9:4-5 CJB)

Question: Why is it so important to understand that
                  Jesus was Jewish?

Chapter Three

Humble King Returning King

"He was despised and rejected by men, a man of sorrows, and familiar with suffering."

Isaiah 53:3 [NIV]

"If we think of Jesus as the Messiah from heaven, the surroundings of outward poverty, so far from detracting, seem most congruous to His Divine character."

Alfred Edersheim

"Therefore God raised him to the highest place and gave him the name above every name; that in honor of the name given Yeshua, every knee will bow – in heaven, on earth and under the earth – and every tongue will acknowledge that Yeshua the Messiah is Adonai – to the glory of God the Father."

Phil. 2:9-11 [CJB]

Chapter Three

Humble King Returning King

Escaping from the burning Middle Eastern sun, we found shelter amidst the trees of a hilltop garden by the Sea of Galilee, not far from where Messiah Jesus spoke the profound words of the Ten Beatitudes recorded in the Gospel of Matthew – the blessings and laws heralding the inauguration of the messianic kingdom. Christians had built a small church to commemorate the site and surrounded it with a serene garden setting. That day as we stopped to pray there was a strong sense of the presence of Jesus in our midst. Perhaps, the uniqueness of that moment was attributable to the fact that we were in the very land of the King surrounded by the places where he lived and taught and performed miracles; seeing with our own eyes the land we had only known before through the words of Scripture, left us expecting the miraculous. There was something transcendent about the land of Israel that went beyond the ancient rocks and desert sands.

Then and now, Israel is a living miracle of the fulfillment of the promises of God. The mystique of Israel is equally the places where in history God's presence touched the earth, as well as a testimony to divine providence in the rebirth of a nation and the return of her people from two thousand years of exile. For a mind submitted to God one can't help but

see the divine hand at work in the history of the Jewish people
and the State of Israel preserving her from her enemies and
gathering her people from the four corners of the earth.
Walking like a guest in a spiritual homeland among the soldiers
and citizens of modern Israel, one senses that this is the Land
and the people from whom and to whom the King first came in
humility, his kingship veiled, and to whom he shall come again
as the returning King (Rom. 11:25-36). The land of Israel is the
Land of the King.

The Humble King

Critics of Christianity have called it a religion for losers
and the weak, but tragically such words betray a chosen
perspective viewed from outside the Kingdom of God;
ultimately, a failure to see the bigger picture. The biblical
accounts of Jesus hold two themes in constant tension. On the
one hand, we are confronted with the humility, weakness,
suffering and rejection of the Messiah; while on the other hand,
his glory, power, authority, and kingship are proclaimed. The
ancient Rabbis saw this distinction in the passages about
Messiah in the Hebrew Scriptures and formulated two
categories of Scripture about the Messiah.[1] The suffering
Messiah of the Prophets was Mashiach Ben-Yosef, Messiah the
Son of Joseph, who like Joseph suffered in Egypt to save the
people of Israel, and the kingly Messiah was Mashiach Ben-
David, Messiah the Son of David, who would rule and reign on

---

[1] For an introductory discussion see: *Encyclopedia Judaica*, 1st ed., s.v.
"Messiah."

the Throne of David forever. The New Testament presents the same contrast. These two opposing views of Messiah must be held in tension to understand the strategic plan of God.

From the very beginning, the kingship of Jesus was veiled in secrecy. This was not an accident. This was the sovereign will of God. He was born in the royal city of Bethlehem, the City of King David, the great Monarch from whom descended a dynasty of Kings, but his birth was not in a royal palace but in a humble stable for his parents could find no other room for the night. Miryam, the mother of Jesus was a modest Jewish virgin, but she was also of royal blood, a descendant of King David. Yosef, the step-father of Jesus, was a simple tradesman, but also a legal heir to the throne of David. Through his mother and step-father, Jesus had a rightful claim to the throne of David. On the night of the birth of the promised King of Israel a great number of angels appeared to herald his birth, but their appearance was only to a few humble shepherds watching their flocks in the fields. From the very beginning Jesus was wrapped in humility and kingship.

It is usually during the Christmas season that we remember the birth of Messiah. Perhaps at no other time of year in the Western World than at Christmas do hopes run highest about universal "peace on Earth and goodwill towards men" (Luke 2:14 KJV). The message of Christmas is told as a message of peace among all people and reconciliation among family and friends. While these sentiments have the appearance of nobility they obscure the ultimate purpose for which the Messiah and King came to the earth. Jesus explained his purpose for coming, but it was the opposite of what was expected of the kingly Messiah. Jesus said, "the Son of Man, came here not to be served but to serve others, and to give my life as a ransom for many" (Matt. 20:28 NLT); these are the words of the suffering Messiah, Mashiach Ben-Yosef. The humble birth, life and humiliating death of Jesus were not the outcome of unfortunate circumstances, but the intended purpose of God to reach down out of love and send his son, Jesus, to save humanity. The ultimate expression of his love for us was the crucifixion. Jesus wasn't crucified by accident it was the very purpose for which the eternal Word of God was born as a man. For this reason when John recorded his vision of the resurrected King in heaven he described him as "a Lamb that had been killed," but was now alive and worshipped in Heaven (Rev. 5:4-8 NLT). The humility of Messiah was the overflow of his divinity and an expression of the compassionate character of God towards all, even those who hated him. This was the high standard that Jesus declared when he said that those who love their enemies and pray for those who hurt them are "acting as children of the Most High" (Luke 6:34 NLT) and displaying the family resemblance of their Father God.

But any notion that peace on earth could arise without conflict is naïve at best. Jesus also said, "do not suppose that I have come to bring peace to the earth. I did not come to bring peace, but a sword" (Matt. 10:34 NLT). By these very words Jesus seemingly contradicted his own command to love our enemies (Matt. 5:44) and his blessing upon the peacemakers (Matt. 5:9). The sword that Jesus spoke of here was not a literal sword, but language masterfully used to convey the deepest of divisions that would occur among those who believed in him as Messiah and those who rejected him. This sword represented the deepest of pain that some of his followers would experience when their very own family would reject them for choosing to follow him, in the same manner that the family of Israel rejected Jesus as the Messiah at his first coming. This sword would draw the spiritual battle lines between the Kingdom of God and the kingdom of darkness inhabited by the enemies of God. This sword reminds us that the Prince of Peace is also the Lord and Commander of the Host of the heavenly army of angels (Josh. 5:13-15; Rev. 19:11-21). Recall that the Armies of Heaven appeared in the skies to the humble shepherds when Jesus was born. The shepherds were surrounded by the radiance of the glory of God and those same humble shepherds were terrified (Luke 2:9). The initial terror of the shepherds was comforted by the words of the angelic messenger who told them not to be afraid for he brought them "good news that will bring great joy to all people. The Savior-yes, the Messiah, the Lord-has been born today in Bethlehem, the city of David!" (Luke 2:10 NLT). This sword also reminds us that Messiah's promised "peace on earth" will only come "to those with whom God is pleased" (Luke 2:14 NLT).

The Returning King

The same King who came in humility will again return, but his return will be very different from his secret birth in Bethlehem. The Armies of Heaven will again appear in the skies, but this time their purpose will not be to announce the good news of the coming of the King. This time the Armies of Heaven will appear following their King to war. It will be terrifying and there will be no angelic messenger to offer words of comfort. The first objectives of the warfare strategy of God were accomplished when Jesus first came to the earth. He came veiled in humility to serve and not be served "and to give his life a ransom for many" (Matt. 20:28 NIV) paying the price for our sin. He lived a perfect life fully obeying the Law of God in complete holiness and absolute sexual purity. He satisfied the wrath of God and once and for all defeated Satan's strangle hold on humanity by breaking the satanic chains that since Adam barred us from paradise. Through the resurrection Jesus defeated death itself so that those who believe in him could "dwell in the house of the Lord forever" (Psalm 23:6 KJV). At his return the King will achieve the final objectives in the warfare against the kingdom of darkness and he will firmly establish the Kingdom of God.

At his return the glory of the kingship of Jesus will not be veiled, but will be the revelation of Mashiach Ben-David, the kingly Messiah. Just as Ezekiel described in his vision of the glory of God in Heaven (Ezek. 1:26-28) the returning King will blaze with the fire of God as his eyes burn with "flames of fire" (Rev. 19:12 NLT). Upon his head his crowns will symbolize his rightful rule and authority as the root and offspring of David (Rev. 22:16) to rule on the Throne of David forever, and with his sword he will strike down the nations (Rev. 19:15). His warfare will be just and his judgment will be true as he unleashes the "fierce wrath of almighty God" (Rev. 19:15 NLT). No one will be spared his wrath among those outside the Kingdom of God. The armies of heaven will appear "dressed in pure white linen" following the King on white horses (Rev. 19:14 NLT). Those who wear pure white linen are the angelic host of heaven and the people of God who during their earthly lives followed the Messiah in suffering and humiliation. When the King returns they too will march out to wage a victorious war with him. There will be no appearance of weakness among the people of God when they return with their King. As foretold by Isaiah:

"The LORD looked and was displeased to find there was no justice. He was amazed to see that no one intervened to help the oppressed. So he himself stepped in to save them with his strong arm...He will repay his enemies for their evil deeds...The redeemer will come to Jerusalem to buy back those in Israel who have turned from their sins, says the LORD" (Is. 59:15-20 NLT).

The return of the King will elicit only two responses. Those who served him and followed Messiah Jesus during their lives will be filled with joy and celebration that the final victory is achieved over the enemies of God, that the Messiah will establish the rule and reign of his messianic Kingdom, and that eternal peace with God is at hand in the new Heavens and the new Earth where "they shall be His people, God Himself will be with them, and be their God" (Rev. 21:3 KJV). Those who did not serve him will have the worst of all possible nightmares realized for "the cowardly, the unbelieving, the vile, the murderers, the sexually immoral, those who practice magic arts, the idolaters and all liars—their place will be in the fiery lake of burning sulfur" (Rev. 21:7-8 NASB). The humble king Jesus is the returning King Messiah.

Main Thought: Jesus is both the humble King who gave his life in our place and the returning King who will wage war and judge those who did not believe in him.

Key Verses: *"That at the name of Jesus every knee will bow, in heaven and on earth and under the earth and every tongue will confess that Jesus Christ is Lord, to the glory of God the Father."* Phil 2:10-11 [NLT]

Questions: Which kingdom do you belong to, the Kingdom of God or the kingdom of darkness?

Chapter Four

The Fire of God

"But who may abide the day of his coming? And who shall stand when he appeareth? For he is like a refiner's fire"

Malachi 3:2 [KJV]

Chapter Four

The Fire of God

There is a fire of God that burns within the hearts and souls of the people of God. At times it is a gentle flame, but then, unexpectedly it transforms into a blazing inferno that burns yet does not consume. It burns and removes everything that would hinder the work of God. Those who experience it fall on their faces before God, filled with awe and godly fear. A burning hunger for holiness and righteousness results from knowing and being known in the intimate presence of God. While it is true that not all know of this fire, it is not the work of human will that ignites the fire of God within the heart, but the work of the sovereign Lord God acting to accomplish his will. This is the fire that Moses encountered in the burning bush. This is the fire that Israel experienced at Sinai. This is the fire in the vision of the glory of God from the prophet Ezekiel. This is the fire that John the Baptist prophesied would characterize Messiah's baptism. This is the fire of God the disciples of Jesus experienced on Shavu'ot. This is the fire of God that falls from heaven upon those who seek God's face.

The Burning Bush

The setting was the desert region of the Sinai Peninsula. Majestic mountains and desert canyons formed a rugged, yet

awe inspiring backdrop for Moses' first encounter with the
God of Abraham, Isaac, and Jacob. This simple shepherd raised
in the household of the mighty Pharaoh of Egypt led his flock
through the wilderness in the course of a normal day's work.
Then off in the distance Moses saw a sight that caught his
attention. A bush burned with fire, yet was not consumed. As
Moses approached, the glory of the Lord surrounded him and
the Lord spoke to him from the midst of the burning bush, "I
am the God of your ancestors. The God of Abraham, the God
of Isaac, and the God of Jacob" (Ex. 3:5 NLT). Moses was
afraid and covered his face.

The Scriptures teach that what Moses saw was not just
a vision or his imagination, but an event that actually
happened. This was the moment that the Lord first spoke to
Moses and revealed the purpose for his life: the liberation of
the People of Israel from slavery in Egypt to life in the
Promised Land. Moses first met the Lord through the burning
bush on the Mountain of God, Mount Horeb, or as it is also
known, Mount Sinai (Ex. 3:1). Moses experienced the presence
of God as a fire that burned, but did not consume.

The Fire of God on Mount Sinai

God did liberate his people Israel from Egypt through
Moses. All of Israel and Egypt witnessed the signs and
wonders of the mighty acts of God. Israel was free and Moses
brought them to the place where it all began: Mount Sinai. The
Lord commanded Moses to tell the people of Israel to purify
themselves and wash their clothes for the Lord would appear to

them on the third day, and the people obeyed (Ex. 19: 10-15). The first time the Lord appeared to Moses it was as a burning bush. But on that particular third day, the Lord would reveal himself in his glory, might, and power upon Mount Sinai.

On the third day, the mountain was alive with the power of God, roaring like a storm of thunder and lightening. As God descended upon Mount Sinai a thick cloud covered the mountain. The people of Israel trembled with fear as Moses led them closer to the mountain. It was as if the entire mountain was on fire. As we read the eyewitness account in Exodus, "smoke billowed into the sky like smoke from a brick kiln, and the whole mountain shook violently...Moses spoke, and God thundered his reply" (Ex. 19:16-19 NLT). The Lord spoke and gave the Law to Israel. Just as with God's revelation of himself in the burning bush, the mountain burned with fire, but was not destroyed. God's glory was first revealed to Moses as a humble burning bush, but on that particular third day, it was a mighty blazing inferno of divine intensity upon Mount Sinai. In both cases, fire was the form which God chose to reveal himself; it was only the magnitude of intensity that changed.

The Fire of God in Ezekiel's Vision of God's glory

An intense revelation of God's presence began the lifework of many of the ancient prophets of Israel, but even among the writers of the Bible very few claimed to have seen an actual vision of the glory of God in Heaven. Ezekiel is one of the few who did. His description of what he saw ends with the words, "this is what the glory of the Lord looked like to me" (Ezek. 1:28 NLT; cf. Ezek. 8:2). Whatever he witnessed was the glory of God. Ezekiel's prophecies and visions from God first began approximately 600 years before Messiah was born (around 593 B.C.E.). The Lord had appeared to Abraham as a man (Gen. 18:1-15), and to Moses as a burning bush, and later to Israel as a mountain alive with the fire of God. But Ezekiel was transported to heaven in a vision and God revealed his glory to him in a unique manner. What is remarkable about Ezekiel's vision is that the glory of God that he witnessed was a figure "whose appearance resembled a man" (Ezek. 1:26 NLT), but a man who like the burning bush and like Mount Sinai burned with fire, but was not destroyed. Ezekiel wrote, "From what appeared to be his waist up, he looked like gleaming amber, flickering like a fire. And from his waist down, he looked like a burning flame shining with splendor…this is what the glory of the Lord looked like to me" (Ezek. 1:27 NLT). Ezekiel's response was to fall on his face before the Lord in submission and adoration.

When the Lord appeared to Moses in the burning bush he revealed himself using the bush, which burned but was not destroyed, as a representation of his glory. Theologians call this a theophany, which means a visible representation of God. This was also what occurred at Mount Sinai on the third day when the Lord gave the Law to Israel. But what Ezekiel saw in his vision was not just a representation of God, but a vision of the very glory of God in heaven, which was a gleaming fire burning brightly with splendor. Ezekiel saw the presence of God, "whose appearance resembled a man" burning intensely with the fire of the glory of the Lord. Ezekiel's vision teaches us that when the veil of our current existence is pulled back and we are given vision to see into the inner sanctuary of Heaven, there we see that truly "our God is a consuming fire" (Heb. 12:29 NASB; cf. Deut. 4:24).

Jesus and the Baptism of Fire

Centuries later the last of Israel's great prophets, John the Baptist (in Hebrew his name is Yochanan) was preparing Israel for the long-awaited coming of the Messiah. He called for the people of Israel to repent of their sins and symbolically wash themselves just like the Lord had commanded Israel at Mount Sinai. John led Israel in the performance of the Jewish ritualistic washing called a mikvah (later translated from the Greek word for immersion as baptism). John the Baptist taught that when the Messiah came he would also baptize, but it would be a baptism with the "Holy Spirit and with fire" (Matt. 3:11 NLT). In the history of Israel, God had consistently revealed the intensity of his glory and presence as fire. John taught that when the long-awaited Messiah would appear, he would wash his people not merely with water, which could only cleanse the outside of a man, but with a washing that would be an immersion in the very presence of God, the baptism of fire.

During the earthly ministry of Jesus, before his death and resurrection, we read nothing of the fire of God or a baptism of fire. This changed dramatically after Messiah was crucified and rose from the dead. We read in the Gospel of Luke that after Jesus rose from the dead he appeared to two of his disciples on the road to a small town in the Northern part of Israel called Emmaus. Jesus' identity was hidden from these two disciples as he taught them about himself from the Hebrew Scriptures (the Old Testament). After Jesus revealed himself to them as the risen Messiah and left them, the disciples in amazement said, "didn't our hearts burn within us as he talked with us on the road and explained the Scriptures to us?" (Luke 24:32 NLT). The prophesy of John the Baptist was only now beginning to be fulfilled, a foreshadowing of the baptism of the Messiah that would wash his disciples with the intense glory of God experienced in their hearts as fire.

Exactly fifty days after Passover, when Messiah Jesus had been crucified, his Jewish disciples and followers had gathered together in one place in Jerusalem (Acts 2:1) to celebrate the ancient Hebrew festival of Shavu'ot, also known as Pentecost because it falls on the 50th day after Passover (counting begins after the first night). Shavu'ot celebrates God's provision and redemption. Historically, the first fruits from the harvest were brought as offerings to God in the ancient Temple in Jerusalem. Shavu'ot is also the celebration of the giving of the Law at Sinai. On that particular Shavu'ot in 30 C.E., suddenly and unexpectedly a sound like a rushing windstorm roared around the disciples and God's glory appeared and descended upon them all in the form of fire (Acts 2:2-4). Just like at Mount Sinai, God's glory was revealed with the sounds of a storm and with fire, but this time the fire of God descended not upon a bush or a mountain, but upon the believers themselves chosen from among the family of Israel. Like the burning bush, the fire of God burned upon them, but they were not consumed. The fulfillment of the prophesy of John the Baptist had begun and the promised Messiah of Israel,

Jesus, was pouring out his baptism with the Ruach HaKodesh – the Holy Spirit – and with fire.

The accounts of the fire of God that burned at Sinai and that filled the disciples of Messiah Jesus on that particular Shavu'ot are not merely stories upon the pages of an ancient book. Ezekiel's vision of the glory of God was a vision of the Messiah whose origins are "from the days of eternity" (Mic. 5:2 NASB) and who is "the image of the invisible God" (Col. 1:15 NLT). Messiah Jesus walked the earth in humility, but now sits upon the Throne of David at the Father's right hand and his appearance is that of a "burning flame shining with splendor" (Ezek. 1:27 NLT). This same baptism of fire burns in the hearts of the followers of Messiah Jesus today as it did in the ancient Temple where the Sh'kinah – the manifest presence of God – burned in holiness. As the Apostle Paul wrote, "don't you know that your body is a temple for the Ruach HaKodesh who lives inside you, whom you received from God?" (1 Cor. 6:19 CJB). Recall that the Apostle Paul was also known as Rabbi Shaul (his Hebrew name) and was raised and educated as a rabbi in the Pharisaic tradition at the feet of the Rabbi Gamaliel (Gamaliel the Elder), grandson of the great Rabbi Hillel (Acts 22:3). Paul himself worshipped at the temple before and after he became a follower of Messiah Jesus and he clearly understood the implication of his words.

It is the fire of God that sustains us in our faith and burns the holy Law upon our hearts redeeming us from idolatry to righteousness. The fire of God reveals the intense, holy presence of the Lord within the heart and soul. The fire of God burns away sin and shame and guilt. The fire of God purifies.

The fire of God is the very glory of God, the presence of Messiah Jesus, King of Israel, living within those who believe through the anointing of the Holy Spirit of God upon their souls.

Main thought: There is a fire of God that we can experience in our hearts and souls through the Holy Spirit.

Key Verse: *"I baptize you with water for repentance. But after me will come one who is more powerful than I, whose sandals I am not fit to carry. He will baptize you with the Holy Spirit and with fire."* Matt. 3:11 [NLT]

Question: What is the significance of God revealing himself as fire to Moses and Israel and Jesus baptizing his followers with the Holy Spirit and with fire?

Chapter Five

The Word of God

"Jesus answered, "It is written: 'Man does not live on bread alone, but on every word that comes from the mouth of God.'"

Matt. 4:4 [NIV]

"When you have read the Bible, you will know it is the word of God, because you have found it the key to your own heart, your own happiness and your own duty."

Woodrow Wilson,
28th President of the
United States

"I admit I read the Bible with great love and deep admiration."

David Ben-Gurion,
1ˢᵗ Prime Minister of the
State of Israel

Chapter Five

The Word of God

The words of Messiah Jesus echo across the centuries: "I did not come to abolish the Law of Moses or the writings of the prophets. No, I came to fulfill them. I assure you, until heaven and earth disappear, even the smallest detail of God's law will remain until its purpose is achieved" (Matt. 5:17-18 NLT). There is no alternative means or new media to replace the word of God. Messiah himself taught that the written revelation of God is the very center of life and faith for the people of God – the people of God are the "People of the Book." Uncompromising devotion and obedience to the Scriptures as the standard defining faith and action, preaching and goodness is what distinguishes the true people of God.

The heavens declare the glory of God and in the mystery and wonder of creation our acknowledgment of the Lord as Creator requires a mind of faith and a heart of worship. The Holy Scriptures take what is experienced as wonder and awe in response to the universe around us and declare the nature of God and how we are to worship him. While the words of the Scriptures were written by men they derive not from their own genius, but were given to them by God himself. The signature of God "thus says the Lord" is written all over his word. God gave his word for a purpose. The word of God

79

teaches us about God and records the history of the people of God. It instructs us how to please God, and in Messiah, is God himself revealed. Faith is required to receive the revelation of God in creation, but both faith and obedience are required to receive the revelation of God in the Holy Scriptures.

The Inspiration of the Word of God

There is a perfect unity between the revelation of God in creation and the revelation of God in the Holy Scriptures. It is the same God whose glory is declared in the heavens that inspired men to write the words found in the Holy Scriptures, the words passed on from generation to generation for thousands of years. The inspiration of the Bible was not of the same quality as other writings in human history for we read that it was the Lord himself who spoke and gave men his message to share with the world.

Moses was a meek man (Num. 3:3) and he did not presume that what he had to say was worthy of being heard. It was through such a man as Moses that God chose to speak. The Lord said to Moses, "I will help you speak and will teach you what to say" (Ex. 4:11 NIV). And the Lord spoke through Moses to the people of Israel, to Pharaoh, and through the Law to the whole world. The Lord testifies to his word and it is the appointed medium to pour out his gift of faith into the world (Rom. 10:17). The message is clear, God is and he has spoken, and we can know him. This knowledge of God is objective, precise, specific, and not dependent on feelings or experiences, mystical or otherwise. This is what makes the Holy Bible unique.

Time and time again as the prophets were called by God to speak they responded with fear, meekness, and humility. Like Moses, Jeremiah replied to the Lord, "Ah, Sovereign LORD," I said, "I do not know how to speak; I am only a child" (Jer. 1:6 NIV). The Lord did not respond in anger or rebuke, but strengthened his prophet and emboldened him with the mission that, "'you must go to everyone I send you to and say whatever I command you. Do not be afraid of them, for I am with you and will rescue you,' declares the Lord" (Jer. 1:7-8 NIV). The means of inspiration to the prophet was received directly from God himself, not through some medium or ecstatic experience: "the LORD reached out his hand and touched my mouth and said to me, 'Now, I have put my words in your mouth...I am with you, and I will take care of you. I, the Lord, have spoken!" (Jer. 1:9; 19 NIV). No prophet of the Lord became suicidal or depressed because of their encounter with the living God, their suffering was a result of the rejection of their message by the people of Israel (Jer. 18: 18-23, etc.).

The inspiration of the Scriptures was never a vague sentimental feeling or subjective impulse. It wasn't motivated by "an act of human will" but "men moved by the Holy Spirit spoke from God" (2 Pet. 1:21 NASB). The Ruach HaKodesh – the Holy wind or spirit of God moved upon the hearts and souls of the men who wrote the Bible and it is the Spirit of God that keeps the Holy Scriptures "alive and powerful" (Heb. 4:12 NLT). Millions of people around the planet open the pages of the Scriptures to draw closer to God and know who he is. The word of God is also called the "sword of the Spirit" (Eph. 6:17) for it cuts "deep into our innermost thoughts and desires" and exposes "us for what we really are" (Heb. 4:11 NLT), one moment convicting, the other comforting; it is through the Bible that God speaks to us personally. This is the most reasonable explanation for why the Bible is pre-eminent among all other books in human history, a "best-seller" to this very day. It was revealed to men in history, but it is kept alive by the Spirit of God. Why else would a book written thousands of years ago still speak so powerfully to our generation? For the believer, the answer is that God himself speaks through the Bible, but for the skeptic, this question remains unanswered.

The Purpose of the Word of God

Without the word of God we would only know of God's existence – "his eternal power and divine nature" (Rom. 1: 20 NLT), but we would never actually know who he is. Without God's word, we would be like children who were given gifts our whole lives from a father who was absent and unknown because he never signed a card, wrote a letter, or bothered to make the effort to actually tell his children who he was and that he loves us. A god who would create a world but never identify himself would be infinitely cruel. But the Lord God wants us to know him and love him. The purpose of the word of God is to teach us who God is and instruct us how to live righteously (2 Tim. 3:16-17). This is why the Scriptures teach that the Law of God is like a school teacher (Gal. 3:24) instructing us what to do and what not to do. The literal meaning of the biblical word "law" is instruction (Hebrew 'torah'). God gave us his word to teach us. The natural place to start with learning about God is creation and so the Scriptures teach that "the heavens declare the glory of God" (Ps. 19:1 KJV), but to fully understand how to please the Lord and know him we must study the Scriptures for it is the "law of the LORD" that is "perfect" and restores our souls (Ps. 19:7 NASB) to a state like Adam and Eve in the Garden of Eden.

It is the word of God that gives us the wisdom to know how to live (Ps. 19:7) and in believing and obeying it we will find a deep sense of contentment, peace, and fulfillment in the core of our being (Ps. 19:8, cf. Jam. 1:22). The word of God is so pure and holy that when it lives within our souls the darkness of our lives is banished and our eyes shine brightly with sight (Ps. 19:8), like the face of Moses after he descended from the presence of the Lord on Sinai. We are cleansed by obedience to God's word in this life, and our obedience has eternal ramifications (Ps. 19:9). The word of God declares to us the judgments of the Lord God, the Divine Judge over all of humanity, and reveals his judgments as absolute Truth and irreversible, but completely righteous, just, and fair (Ps. 19:9). The Bible records for us the history of the people of God who through their faith in the Lord fought intense battles and achieved victories to the glory of the Lord and are the "witnesses to the life of faith" to inspire us to endure and run "the race that God has set before us" (Heb. 12:1 NLT). This is the purpose of God's Word.

The response of the people of God to the Bible covers the spectrum of human experience. At times the Lord speaks through his word to fill the heart with the deepest joy and peace known to humanity and to imprint upon the soul the same glory that he displays in the skies. For the believer, the Scriptures are an anchor in a world suffering from uncertainty about how to live and what to believe as truth. Some days it exposes the darkness in our lives, brings the conviction of sin, and pierces with the terror of judgment; the believer trembles before the word of God (Is. 66:2, 5). But then, like an unexpected gift from a loving father, we rejoice before God through his word (Ps. 119:162). There is an earthy grounding in the soil of the earth when the peace of God enters our soul through the very words God himself inspired, like traveling back in time to ancient Israel and breathing in the divine presence under the Mediterranean sky. The worship of God and the word of God are intimately connected, for in his word God has revealed his character and glory. It is not just the sentences and words, phrases and paragraphs of the Scriptures, but the very one who moved and inspired the prophets of God who actually speaks to our souls through his word; a perfect unity of the experience of the subjective and spiritual with the objective and rational, with no chasm between sacred and secular.

The Word Enters Human History

The message given to the prophets of the Lord was always given from God and the prophet was merely the appointed messenger. As Jeremiah wrote, 'the Lord reached out and touched my mouth" (Jer. 1:9 NLT) and then Jeremiah became a prophet. But something remarkable happened in that stable in Bethlehem 2000 years ago, not just a prophet was born, but the very one who inspired the prophets and gave his words to them himself took on human form to reveal God to us like no mere words could convey. John explained it like this:

"in the beginning the Word already existed. He was with God, and he was God. He was in the beginning with God...so the Word became human and he lived here on earth among us. He was full of unfailing love and faithfulness. And we have seen his glory, the glory of the only Son of the Father" (John 1:1-5, 14 NLT).

Not surprisingly when the one who inspired the prophets himself spoke and gave his message the response of the people of Israel was that he taught with "real authority," and had a quality unlike the religious teachers of his day (Matt. 7:28-29 NLT). The words of Jesus are at one and the same time eternally wise and deeply human. Atheists and disciples both are silenced and drawn to him.

The Sermon on the Mount

It is in the introductory words of Messiah's Sermon on the Mount (Matt. 5-7), that we find summarized the universal problems that reach the existential depths of life; nine blessings and one final tenth commandment. First, we find the problem of injustice and oppression (Matt. 5:3), and next the problem of suffering (Matt. 5:4). Two promises, but what are the deeper questions to which these answers are given? These words were not intended as abstract wisdom echoing the divine in white marble temples upon the platonic clouds of heaven. These blessings were given in a specific context, rooted in the soil of the earth. To unlock their meaning we must think like Messiah's audience in the 1st century. And so we find the key in the third blessing.

In biblical and rabbinical literature, the number three was used to indicate the divine will or emphasis. For example, it was on the third day that God showed Abraham where to offer Isaac in the near-sacrifice (Gen. 22:3-4), on the third day God appeared to Israel at Sinai (Ex. 19:16), and on the third day Jesus rose from the dead (Luke 18:31-33). The Gospel of Matthew was written for a Jewish audience familiar with the biblical tradition of numbers and their meanings, and they were living in expectation of the physical, messianic kingdom to be brought into power by the Messiah (Acts 1:6). So it is in the third pronouncement of messianic blessing that we find something deeper, below the surface that, in this emphatic third placement, elevates its importance to unlock the questions behind the blessings in this sermon of answers: "Blessed are the meek for they shall inherit the land" (Matt. 5:5), a direct quote taken from Psalm 37:11 (cf. Ps. 37: 3, 9, 27, 29, 34), and reference to the ancient promise to inherit the land, the Land of Israel.[1] It is here that Messiah gives his audience the context to

---

[1] In this verse, 'the land' in the Greek is *'ten gen.'* This can be translated as the earth, land, ground, or country. In the parallel verse in Ps. 37:11, *'the land'* is a translation of *'ha eretz'*. Today, Israel and 'Ha Eretz' (The Land) are used synonymously to refer to the modern State of Israel following the biblical tradition. A principle of biblical interpretation is that the author usually intended only one meaning for each word he chose. The reference to Israel (the land) is what most reasonably the author had in mind, and also how his 1st century Jewish readers would most likely have understood it.

his words and the treasury in which to search for the questions behind his answers of blessing: the Tehillim, the Psalms, the prayers of Israel.

Messiah's blessing and promise that the meek and humble would inherit the land was and is the deepest hope of the Jewish soul, the longing to live in safety and peace in the land of Israel. But not just to live in the land promised to Abraham, Isaac, Jacob and their descendants, but to dwell there with the divine presence in the midst of his people, to be the Kingdom of God (compare Gen. 12:1-3; Ex. 19:6; 2 Sam. 7:10-11; 1 Kings 8:10) and see his presence and promises fulfilled. In this third messianic blessing, Messiah reiterates the promise of the Kingdom of God – the Kingdom of Heaven,[2] the hope of Israel; for the meek *shall* inherit *the Land*. In Messiah's words, we find the universal longing of humanity to know and see God, not only in hope and faith, but to know him fully just as he knows us (1 Cor. 13:12) and cross the barrier between the seen and the unseen, and to see God with our own eyes in our human bodies. As Solomon prayed when he dedicated the Temple with joyful disbelief of hope realized of the inheritance of the land of Israel and God's presence, "will God really live on the earth? Why, even the highest heavens cannot contain you. How much less this Temple I have built!" (1 Kings 8:27 NLT), and the "glorious presence of the Lord filled the Temple" (1 Kings 8:11 NLT).

But life in the Kingdom was universally lost in Eden due to Adam's sin, and so the fourth blessing is upon those

---

[2] The Kingdom of God and the Kingdom of Heaven are used interchangeably in the Gospel of Matthew.

who hunger and long to know goodness and righteousness once again in their lives and in those around them, and to this desire he promises satisfaction and fulfillment (Matt. 5:6; cf. Ps. 37:5-6, 25). Righteousness was the condition the Lord placed on Solomon for the continued presence of the Sh'kinah in the Temple and God's visible, manifest protection over Israel's inheritance of the land (1 Kings 9:3-9). Through the Prophet Jeremiah, the Lord reiterated the promise to "the house of Israel and the house of Judah" to make them his kingdom, and his unconditional acceptance, even in the face of their sin, under the terms of the New Covenant (Jer. 31:31-37). The promise of the land to Abraham and his descendants through Isaac and Jacob, was a promise made with no conditions attached (Gen. 12:1-3); God always protects Israel even when his presence seems absent, as we read in the story of Queen Esther, where there is no mention of God in the narrative.[3] It is in the New Covenant that the Lord himself out of love for Israel, promised to take it upon himself to insure that Israel would fulfill the Lord's call to righteousness to live in the Kingdom of God. Living in the land was unconditional, but the removal of the cursing of enemies and the continuation of the presence of God was conditional upon righteousness (1 Kings 9:6-9; cf. Ps. 51:10-11, written after David committed adultery with Bathsheba).

---

[3] The religious calendar of Judaism is a lunar based calendar. The story of Queen Esther is commemorated every year at Purim and falls on the first full moon before Passover, which falls on the following full moon. Passover celebrates the Lord's visible redemption and deliverance of Israel from Egypt into the promised Kingdom of God in Canaan. These two festivals are a reminder of God's protection and deliverance, both unseen and visible.

The reality of the world is that those who seek goodness, who seek to live in the Kingdom of God, will be oppressed by the wicked, and so his fifth blessing reminds his hearers that it is the merciful who will be shown mercy (Matt. 5:7; cf. Ps. 37:30-31).

A wicked world hardens the soul and darkens the heart with its bitterness, so the sixth blessing offers the hope of innocence, purity, and safety in the presence of God (Matt. 5:8; cf. Ps. 37:18, 39-40), for those who are pure in heart will see God in their human bodies – Solomon's hope; six is the number of man for on the sixth day God created humanity.

The longing for peace when surrounded by those who bring destruction is an ancient song of prayer offered to the Lord by Israel as they ascended to Jerusalem to worship at the Temple (Ps. 120), and so Messiah's seventh blessing is upon those who work for peace. Not in the absence of conflict, but through the midst of it, as he also suffered much to bring peace. Those who seek after peace will themselves be called children of God (Matt. 5:9); seven is the number of God and on the seventh day God rested.

But just as Messiah suffered to bring peace, just as Joseph suffered to save Israel from famine in Canaan, just as Daniel suffered for his devotion to God, even as an advisor and statesman in ancient Babylon, so all those will suffer who seek the Kingdom of God through righteousness (Matt. 6:33). Those who live with the hope that one day they will inherit the physical Kingdom of God on earth, an Israel of peace, will suffer persecution (Matt. 5:10-12). Often the cost of peace is paid in suffering, persecution, sacrifice, and death, but this eighth blessing offers the eternal hope of inheriting the Kingdom of Heaven.

The ninth blessing intensifies the persecution that will come upon those who follow Messiah. It will mean being lied about, mocked, slandered, and oppressed, but their suffering is the evidence that God's blessing is upon them.

In the tenth position, we find not a blessing, but the command to rejoice for those who have been counted worthy to suffer rejection, persecution, and even death, are just like the ancient prophets of Israel. The rest and reward of the Kingdom of God remains. 'L'shanah haba b'Yerushalayim'[4] – 'Next Year in Jerusalem' for 'Jerusalem' means the city of the 'heritage of peace'. "Jerusalem is the city of the great King" (Matt. 5:35 NLT) and is the symbol of the hope of the Kingdom of God on the earth; the meek shall inherit the land.

Eternal above His Word

His words were recorded in the Scriptures, but there is no actual image or likeness of Jesus for God commanded not to make images *or* symbols to worship; "you must not make for yourself an idol of any kind or an image...you must not bow down to them or worship them, for I, the Lord your God am a jealous God" (Ex. 20:4-5 NLT); God has always chosen to reveal himself through his word. And it is for this reason that

---

[4] "L'shanah haba b'Yerushalayim" is an ancient Hebrew melody sung after the Passover Seder (meal) and after Yom Kippur. The theme of hope is also found in the national anthem of Israel, "Hatikvah," which is literally translated as "the Hope," is the hope to be a free people in the land.

Jesus entered human history when his life and words were recorded and written down into what we now know as the New Covenant (New Testament) Scriptures. It was not by accident that Jesus was born before television, photography, and film, for the Lord God has always revealed himself through his word. The moments when the divine presence touched the earth in the history of Israel are recorded in the Scriptures, from Abraham to the kings to the prophets, but the Lord God is eternal above his word. In the same way, when the eternal word became flesh, Messiah Jesus, he revealed his glory to the world among his own family, Israel, but today, his glory is revealed through the words of the Scriptures.

How then shall we live?

If we have chosen to believe and follow, then the word of God must be central to our lives, not just a select passage or verse, but "every word that comes from the mouth of God (Matt.4:4 NASB; cf. Deut. 8:3). And if we claim to be the people of God and followers of Messiah Jesus, but do not obey the word of God we are fooling ourselves (Luke 8:21) for the blessing of God is upon those who both "hear the word of God and observe it" (Luke 11:28 NASB). Those who claim to love the Lord, even love Jesus, but do not love and obey the word of God are self-deceived and worship a false God. The word of God is the eternal standard of truth and righteousness and the word of God revealed is Messiah Jesus.

Main thought: The word of God was uniquely inspired and given by God to teach us who he is and how we ought to live to please him.

Key Verse: *"Jesus answered, "It is written: 'Man does not live on bread alone, but on every word that comes from the mouth of God.'"*

Questions: What place does the word of God occupy in your life? Is it central and foundational to guiding your faith and behavior? Or do you treat it as secondary to your personal experiences, beliefs, and feelings?

Part II:

Walking by Faith

Chapter Six

Ambition and Faithfulness

"Make it your ambition to lead a quiet life, to mind your own business and to work with your hands, just as we told you."

1 Thessalonians 4:11 [NIV]

Chapter Six

Ambition and Faithfulness

Ambition and calling are distinct, but intertwined. Ambition gives us our perspective, our objectives, and our goals. Calling is what we must do because it is the purpose for which we have been created. Twisted minds have twisted ambition and twisted calling based not on the fear of God, goodness, righteousness, and justice, but based on self-interest, selfish-gain, and pleasure at all costs. There was once a time when a man was defined by his commitment, to what is faithful like a farmer who works hard to harvest his crops to provide for his family, to self-sacrifice for freedom as embodied in the values of a soldier, and to self-discipline and perseverance like an athlete. Society still praises these virtues, but they are no longer ingrained into our generation as the foundation of character, goodness, and nobility.

Our ambition should be to lead a quiet life as Paul wrote to the ancient church in Thessalonica. This should be the foundation that underlies everything we do. Ambition should never be for greatness. If greatness becomes our ambition then we will lose the integrity that is the substance of true greatness. We have control over what we make our ambition, but we cannot control our calling; "In his heart a man plans his course, but the Lord directs his steps" (Prov. 16:9 NIV). If our ambition is rooted in the wisdom of God and the soil of the earth, then regardless of our calling, our perspective will be correct.

The ideal of the quiet life is embodied in the ambition to be a man of God, with strength of moral character, to be a husband, who loves and protects his wife, and to be a father, who raises his sons and daughters with wisdom and instills in them a yearning for nobility. These are the greatest gifts from God; "Your wife will be like a fruitful vine within your house; your sons will be like olive shoots around your table. Thus is the man blessed who fears the LORD" (Ps. 128:3-4 NIV).

I heard the tragic story of a family friend. His son proudly served his country in Iraq with the Army and returned home safe and healthy to his wife and daughter. Having risked his own life in the name of freedom and survived he returned home only to discover that his wife had been unfaithful to him. The betrayal and pain was overwhelming and cut deep into him, and in his despair he killed his wife and took his own. The joyful homecoming turned into tragedy. A proud father crumpled in sorrow, his son lost forever. There is nothing that destroys more than unfaithfulness.

Faithfulness is probably one of the rarest of the moral virtues. The ambition of the quiet life is built on faithfulness, but it cannot be bought or earned, it can only be given. It is something both husband and wife give to each other, but when it is violated it destroys.

We live in a hypocritical society. Men and women both want a faithful spouse, but they schizophrenically sleep around with whomever they want whenever they want or can before marriage, and some even after. Sex is treated like fast-food. It is not my place to condemn, but there is a better life.

There was only one perfect man, Messiah Jesus. He set the standard high, "be perfect, even as your Father in heaven is perfect" (Matt. 5:48 NLT). We must desire and strive to please God, but unlike Jesus, the rest of us are all sinners. I've had my share of stupid mistakes, but I can also testify that what is impossible with man is possible with God. The Lord God wrote his laws upon my heart (Jer. 31:33) and the commitment to being sexually faithful to my future wife was built into the foundation of my character way before puberty. Unwisely, I started dating when I was around 13. I don't recommend this for two reasons: ex-girlfriends make the worst enemies (I've collected a few enemies), and second, sexual attraction and desire between a man and a woman is a burning fire like no other, once it's started, you can't play with fire and not get burned. What I'm talking about is sexual impurity, even though there is grace that overcomes guilt, sin, and shame.

I'm not perfect just like you, but I can also testify to the truth that God honors the desire to keep his commandments. When the quiet life is your ambition and ideal from childhood you pray for a godly wife and the Lord answers that prayer with a love for a woman that you've never met that is so powerful that at the very bed of temptation you find the strength to resist burning desire. I'm not talking about "I did not have sex with that woman" a.k.a. former President Clinton. I'm talking about God giving the strength to not give into sex of any kind outside of marriage for the sake of faithfulness. We will fail if we think we can do it (or actually not do it) without God's help, but if we ask God he will give a way to attain to the quiet life, to achieve faithfulness and provide a way out of temptation (1 Cor. 10:12-13).

God's purposes aren't always clear and it's ironic that some of my friends who slept around in high school and college are married and have kids and I'm still praying and looking for that one woman among the many who is "worth far more than rubies." I think I've earned the right to say that she is the rarest of jewels - one among billions.

I've always been a Jacob and never an Isaac. If an angel of destruction comes in my path I'll wrestle and defeat the darkness by God's grace. If an army rises against me I'll fight and defeat it with the help of God. If I have to walk on water to follow Jesus then I'll do it. But sometimes the Lord says, "my Jacob be an Isaac," and this is the toughest assignment he's ever given me. Where Jacob wrestled, Isaac waited. When Jacob met Rachel he moved the stone from the well and gave water to her father's camels. When Isaac met Rebekkah he was out in the fields praying and Rebekkah showed up with the camels, the camels that she gave water to when Eliezer found her at the well. I figured maybe that's the point that I should just hang out in my backyard and pray, pray for the Lord to move in his time, pray for an Eliezer, pray for my Eve, and wait. And I wait.

Waiting and praying. I've always prayed that I would be a godly man whom my future father-in-law would respect and trust with his daughter and as I've prayed over these last few months I've wondered, what are the final obstacles in our path? I don't know what sacrifice her father and mother have to make, but perhaps the cost is high. Perhaps the stakes are higher than I realize. While I may have much to offer, our faith in Jesus, hers and mine, may have consequences that I don't fully understand. A father's respect for a future son-in-law may not be enough to overcome, but a father's love for his daughter can overcome any obstacle; "greater love has no one than this, that he lay down his life for his friends" (John 15:13 NIV)...how much more so for his own daughter, and in my case, for my future wife.

This leaves only faith and faithfulness. If I knew where to go I would go. If I knew what to do I'd do it. But all I can do is pray and trust that when the time is right she will smile in my direction so I can find her and I know she'll know when and what that means and so will I. When you pray for a divinely arranged marriage the Lord answers big time so I figure I'll just keep praying for my Eshet-Chayil[1] and wait while the Lord asks her if this is what she really wants and my Father in heaven negotiates the deal with her father. Maybe this is all crazy, but that's the risk of faith: "Unless the Lord builds a house, the work of the builders is wasted" (Ps 127:1 NLT)...the righteous are never forsaken (Ps. 37:25).

Those who want faithfulness in their husband or wife must be faithful now. If you've messed up make the commitment before God to be faithful starting today. And if you are living the faithful life, then know that God's blessing is with you. His promise to you is that the rare blessing of passion and faithfulness will fill your home (Ps. 128:3).

---

[1] 'Virtuous wife' (Prov. 31:10).

The Nature of Faith

"If I find in myself a desire which no experience in this world can satisfy, the most probable explanation is that I was made for another world."

C.S. Lewis

"For it is by grace you have been saved, through faith—and this not from yourselves, it is the gift of God."

Eph. 2:8-9 [NLT]

Chapter Seven

The Nature of Faith

There are a lot of misconceptions about faith. Some say faith is a blind leap. Others say that faith requires intellectual suicide and is for the naïve and gullible. But real faith is never blind, naïve, or gullible, and it thrives upon a foundation of intellectual humility. The kind of faith that pleases God is the deep, heartfelt, eyes-wide-open faith that sees and accepts the reality of life, but perseveres in trusting God even when the circumstances of life don't give rise or reason to even hope (Rom. 4:18 NLT). This kind of faith acknowledges that life is filled with the conflict between love and hate, hope and disappointment, joy and suffering, peace and war, truth and lies, good and evil, and it chooses to live through the midst of the tension.

Like a soldier left behind enemy lines moving into position to be rescued, confident that he will not be left behind because he knows that others will give even their lives if required to bring him home, true biblical faith never gives up hope, but stubbornly persists in belief and obedience, knowing that God will save; the evidence of deep confidence in the character of God. This kind of faith is always a gift from God that he chooses to place within the human heart, soul, and mind, given to those who seek after him. And to those who seek, they find that life is lived between two worlds, this present world and the eternal Kingdom of God.

Faith is a gift

The place to begin to understand the nature of faith is acknowledging that faith is a gift from God. The Scriptures state this clearly, "for it is by grace you have been saved, through faith—and this not from yourselves, it is the gift of God— not by works, so that no one can boast" (Eph 2:8-9 NIV). It is God's grace – his loving kindness – that saves us and the way he saves us is through faith that arises within us but does not originate from us. This truth has profound implications about how we are to view ourselves and God.

Our natural human tendency is to think that we can save ourselves. That deep down if we made the right choices and responded in the right way our lives would be better. This sentiment is expressed in sayings like "God helps those who help themselves" or "life is 10% what happens to you and 90% how you respond to it." Ultimately, such an attitude places the responsibility for our lives and our future on no one else but ourselves. It follows the reasoning that if our lives are successful and happy then we are the ones who get the credit, but if we are failures and suffer then we are the ones to blame. Such belief is self-centered. The Scriptures paint a very different picture.

The Scriptures teach that we can't pull ourselves up by our boot straps and that God doesn't help those who help themselves. We often think that in any situation we find ourselves we can get out of it, if we put enough effort into it; we think of ourselves as our own gods and messiahs, our own saviors. God calls this idolatry. The correct view is that we are so desperately sinful that if "life is 10% what happens to you" then left to ourselves 100% of the time we will respond in the wrong manner. As it is written, "the human heart is most deceitful and desperately wicked. Who really knows how bad it is? But I know! I, the LORD, search all hearts and examine secret motives. I give all people their due rewards, according to what their actions deserve" (Jer. 17:9-10 NLT).

Left to ourselves, independent of God we are always going to make the wrong choices. That is why we need a Messiah. That is why God gave us his Law. Some might say this is a very low view of humanity, but it isn't. We have great potential for good within us, but left alone we are trapped in our own darkness and evil. This is why Messiah Jesus came to earth to save us, to wipe clean from the record our every violation of God's Law, and enable God to write his Law upon our hearts (Jer. 31:31), so that we could reach the potential for goodness and righteousness that we long for and be pleasing to God and know and feel that he is pleased with us; this *is* salvation, this *is* living in the Kingdom of God. This is where we find the power to actually do good things – the things that God planned for us to do long before we even existed, even before he made the world (Eph. 1:4-5; 2:10).

The crucial thing to understand about salvation and faith is that God is totally in control. No one who is truly good and righteous can take credit for their own salvation (Eph. 2:8). The irony is that those who pride themselves on their salvation or righteousness or good lives, whether they are religious or not, are the very ones who from God's perspective aren't even counted among his people (Matt. 23:27-28). No matter how strong our commitment to righteousness no one is without sin, and if we say so we are a liar (1 John 1:8). When we believe in Messiah's sacrifice to atone for our sins what takes place is that we are forgiven and cleansed from the unrighteousness that polluted our soul (1 John 1:9); God wipes the record clean. But there is a moment when one first believes that we are changed, both in our hearts through the Ruach haKodesh (Holy Spirit), and also in God's eyes. We become children of God or as Messiah told Rabbi Nicodemus, "born again" (John 3:3 NLT). This is when the fire of God is first planted in our hearts, even if in God's time it may burn even stronger or diminish into a calm flame of righteousness; "the wind blows wherever it wants" (John 3:8 NLT). When we first believe the Lord draws close to us. It is as if the Angel guarding the path to the Garden of Eden has lowered his sword and we once again enjoy the purity and intimacy of the Garden of Eden shared between Adam and Eve and the Lord God. This salvation is God's gift and completely the work of God and the greatest evidences of faith are humility and the desire to please God – to fear him. As the tax collector cried out, "O God, be merciful to me, for I am a sinner" (Luke 18:13 NLT), and as the righteous sang on their ascent to Jerusalem, "Lord, if you kept a record of our sins, who, O Lord, could ever survive? But you offer forgiveness, that we might learn to fear you" (Ps. 130:3-4 NLT).

Faith is believing and doing

There is an ancient story of a humble shepherd who chose the best of his firstborn lambs and presented it to the Lord as a gift. It was accepted and he was found righteous in God's eyes. His brother, a farmer, reaped his harvest and also presented some of his crops as a gift to the Lord, but his gift was not accepted. The farmer was disturbed that the Lord had accepted his brother's gift, but rejected his. His bitterness consumed him and in a cold and calculated manner he planned and carried out the murder of his brother, the humble shepherd.

This is, of course, the story of Cain and Abel, the sons of Adam. Abel was a righteous man and offered "the best of the firstborn lambs from his flock" to God (Gen. 4:4 NLT) and his "offering gave evidence that he was a righteous man, and God showed his approval of his gifts" (Heb. 11:4 NLT). Cain, on the other hand, was an ungodly man and his life and offering evidenced that he did not seek after God. Cain's gift was just from "some of his crops" neither the best nor the first of his harvest (Gen. 4:3 NLT). When his gift was rejected Cain acted in accord with his ungodliness and murdered his brother. The faith of Abel and the sin of Cain were demonstrated by what they did. Our actions demonstrate who we really are and the extent to which we have faith in God or ignore him, as Jesus taught, "just as you can identify a tree by its fruit, so you can identify people by their actions" (Matt. 7:20 NLT).

Between two worlds

The outcome of a God-conscious life is a life lived between two worlds, this present world, which we see with our physical eyes, and the world of eternity and life after death – the eternal Kingdom of God, which we see through the eyes of faith (Eccl. 3:11; Heb. 1:1; 2 Cor. 4:18). The experience of the tension between these two worlds is equal to the depth of faith within us. Abraham was led to the promised land of Canaan, but he lived there as a nomad in tents looking forward to the fulfillment of the promises of God. The same was true for Isaac and Jacob (Heb. 11:9). All throughout the history of the people of God they suffered oppression, abuse, and persecution. Those who trusted in God were tortured, but "placed their hope in the resurrection to a better life" (Heb. 11:35 NLT). Such a life in the here and now seems at times to have neither purpose to those within, nor any appeal to those looking on from without.

In some shape or form every true follower of Messiah Jesus will experience suffering. The purpose of God is not to bring harm to his children, but through testing and suffering to refine their faith and place their focus on God in anticipation of an eternity of righteousness and joy in his presence in the kingdom of God where "they shall be his people, and God himself shall be with them, and be their God" (Rev. 21:3; cf. Ex. 6:7; Lev. 26:12; Jer. 7:23, 11:4, 24:7, 30:22, 31:33, 32:28; Ezek. 11:20, 14:11, 36:28, 37:23, 37:27; Zech. 8:8; 2 Cor. 6:16; Heb. 8:10), and where King Messiah Jesus shall rule on the Throne of David forever (Rev. 22:16; John 18:36). The people of God long for their heavenly homeland and "that is why God is not ashamed to be called their God, for he has prepared a city for them" (Heb. 11: 16 NLT), "the holy city, the new Jerusalem" (Rev. 21:2 NLT). The life lived in this world is the gateway to an eternity with God for those who believe.

From faith to eternity

When faced with eternity the question of whether faith truly lives within us quickly fills the mind and heart. Soldiers facing deployment to an arena of warfare feel the closeness of life and death, but why is it that at a given moment eternal destiny weighs just as heavy upon a waitress facing her morning shift? There is a time when God reveals eternity to the soul with inescapable clarity. The biblical doctrine of the nature of faith is that it is a gift that God chooses to give to whomever he desires (Eph. 2:8-9; John 1:12-13; Matt. 11:25-30; Acts 13:48-49, etc.). Believers and skeptics alike may cry out in protest at this apparent imprisonment of human freewill, but there is unavoidable mystery involved in the tension between human freewill and God's control over human destiny. Eliminating the one to take hold of the other always falls short of the glory of God. Both must be held in tension and this requires the humility of a child (Matt. 18:4) and the endurance of a soldier to live through what we now see "imperfectly as in a cloudy mirror," but will one day see "with perfect clarity," and this is the very core of "faith, hope, and love" (1 Cor. 13:11-13 NLT). A believer cannot take credit for the faith within them for it is a gift from God even though they make the choice to follow the Lord. In fact, without the determined resolve to follow Jesus as Messiah, no matter what the cost, the genuineness of ones faith is questionable. But the new birth as a child of God rests solely upon the will of the Father and it is "a birth that comes from God" (John 1:12 NLT).

For those who do not follow Jesus as Messiah the fear may arise that God has not chosen them to be his children and that they have no part in the eternal family of God. This is actually a healthy fear and one that leads to the very place of salvation. For Jesus said, "Come to me, all of you who are weary and carry heavy burdens, and I will give you rest" (Matt. 11:28 NLT). The invitation of Messiah is open to all. The very desire to believe in him and belong to him is the evidence that the Lord has chosen you to be born into the family of God and granted citizenship in Heaven. The source of faith is the Lord. It is a gift that he gives, but like any gift, what is required of us is the decision to accept it.

Main Thought:

Faith is a gift that God gives to whom he chooses and those who receive it show their faith by a determination to believe in God no matter what obstacles they face.

Key Verse:

"For it is by grace you have been saved, through faith—and this not from yourselves, it is the gift of God— not by works, so that no one can boast." (Eph 2:8-9 NIV)

Question:

If you had to present the evidence of your beliefs and actions before a judge and jury what would the verdict be, a life lived by faith in God or a life lived in unbelief?

Chapter Eight

Loyalty

"He was oppressed, and he was afflicted,
    yet he opened not his mouth;
like a lamb that is led to the slaughter,
    and like a sheep that before its shearers is silent,
so he opened not his mouth."

Isaiah 53:7 [NASB]

Chapter Eight

Loyalty

Often the greatest test of loyalty is silence. Not silence understood as the absence of words, but silence as the absence of the words of betrayal, and silence as the absence of words that would save ourselves at the expense of our loyalty to God, family, friends, or even country. During the time of year when Passover and Resurrection Sunday are celebrated, we think back to the sacrifices offered in silence that brought redemption and freedom and the sacrifices that must never be forgotten.

On Passover night the Lord stretched out his hand of wrath against the enemies of God to deliver his people from their slavery in Egypt and lead them into freedom. The Passover lamb that was sacrificed, its blood painted over the doorposts, saved Israel from God's wrath as he passed over the houses of Israel. The painting of the blood was a silent expression of loyalty to God's commands and hope in his deliverance. The lamb had no choice, but those who sacrificed did.

On a different Passover centuries later the words of the Prophet Isaiah were fulfilled as Messiah Jesus offered himself so that the wrath of God could pass over once again. His loyalty to God and the calling set before him was expressed in silence. "Like a lamb that is led to the slaughter, and like a sheep that before its shearers is silent so he opened not his mouth" (Is. 53:7 NIV); the strength of silence. The Lamb of God offered himself, but just as on that first night thousands of years ago, the silent expression of loyalty to God's deliverance is the prayer that by faith paints the blood of the Lamb of God over our lives so that the wrath of God will pass over both now and on the future day of reckoning. It is an act of choice, of necessity, and of loyalty to the purpose and calling of Messiah.

Loyalty is a rare virtue as history evidences betrayal of a magnitude that is so brutal and so depraved and so calculated that one could question whether there is anything good in humanity. Stories of dehumanization and forgery for survival are like nightmares that haunt like ghostly apparitions. Others tell of tragic accounts that ended in the horrific death of innocent millions, children, families, sons, daughters, husbands, wives, mothers, and fathers. This history is part of the collective memory of all humanity and should give birth to a persistence by all to make sure it never happens again. And it is the responsibility of this generation, whether in word or action, to make sure it never does. But then, when least expected, one still faces the attitudes of apathy and indifference, as if the tragedy of their death, and the path that led there, should be ignored or forgotten. Such an attitude represents loyalty, but to a different cause, and reminds us that loyalty, in and of itself, is an empty virtue without goodness.

Only when moral goodness is the foundation of loyalty does loyalty rise as a true virtue. With such loyalty we can stand strong and resist the greatest evil and overcome. And the devil said, "I will give you the glory of these kingdoms and authority over them...because they are mine to give to anyone I please. I will give it all to you if you will worship me" (Luke 4:6-7 NLT). And Jesus said, "You must worship the Lord your God and serve only him" (Luke 4:8 NLT). Satan claims to have the power to cause kingdoms to rise and fall, but he is the father of lies, and his power is only to corrupt, deceive, and use the kingdoms of this world to carry out his plan of efficient destruction and corrupt all that is good. His false power is often hidden under the guise of institutional legitimacy, but his true nature is evidenced by hatred, evil, and death.

Often so-called greatness and success is determined by the degree to which one bows down to this world and compromises what is right to gain glory and entry into the pantheon of celebrity and to hold the seat of power. Satan is especially quick to offer success, fame, and fortune, to those whose intent is service to God with the purest of motivation. The prayer for success or influence or power or material blessing is all too often answered by Satan to remove the power of God from the messenger. The message may not change and success in the eyes of the world may fill shelves with awards and homes with riches, but the anointing of God is removed from those who bow to Satan. No one can serve two masters, and sadly many among those who claim to serve God betray their loyalty to him, not in their message, but in accepting the rewards of this world or giving in to its temptations. If the soul of the messenger has lost the salt of righteousness (Matt. 5:13), the message has lost its moral authority, and sounds a message of empty words regardless of how perfectly composed. The test is not success or failure, but a willingness to choose to do what is right to please God even when it is obvious that the outcome will be financial loss, rejection, and loss of status. Remember that Jesus taught us over and over again that the one who receives their reward in this life, forfeits it in the life to come for "wherever your treasure is, there the desires of your heart will also be" (Matt. 6:21 NLT).

There is only one standard to test our loyalty to the Lord God and that is loyalty to his Holy Word. This is the loyalty that defied the powers of this world when faced with betraying the Lord to save their own lives and said, "the God whom we serve is able to save us...but even if he doesn't we want to make it clear to you...that we will never serve your gods or worship the gold statue you have set up" (Dan. 3:17-18 NLT). Their loyalty was to the command of the Lord which demanded that "you must not worship any of the gods of neighboring nations" (Deut. 6:14 NLT). This is the one and only standard of success and the true test of loyalty: obedience to God's commands; "if you love me you will obey my commands" (John 14:21; cf. 1 John 2:3; 3:22, 24; 5:3).

This world will offer rewards to those who follow after the Lord to distract them from the calling and purpose set before them. But when the world passes by with their glory and awards it should be a cause to "rejoice and be glad" that God has spared us the temptation of success in the world's eyes (Matt. 5:11-12). Worldly success removes godly anointing. Our prayer should never be for success or influence or prosperity, our prayer should be for anointing -- the anointing of God upon our lives and words and songs and sermons. Jesus the Anointed One – the Mashiach (in Hebrew 'mashiach' means 'anointed') – demonstrated for us the true path of ascent and evidenced the characteristic found in all those who have received the anointing of God: obedience to the command of God; "Not my will, but thine, be done" (Luke 22:42 NLT). Obedience should be written upon our hearts and the doorposts of our home so that we can say, with a heart that is free from the politics and deceit of this world, "I give up everything for you, O Lord Our God." This is the test of our loyalty and its fullest expression.

Chapter Nine

The Valley of the Shadow of Death

"He has brought me into deep darkness, shutting out all light. He has turned against me. Day and night his hand is heavy upon me...He has buried me in a dark place, like a person long dead."

Lamentations 3:2-3, 6 [NLT]

"I have come as a light to shine in this dark world, so that all who put their trust in me will no longer remain in the darkness."

John 12:46 [NLT]

Chapter Nine

The Valley of the Shadow of Death

Within the darkness, in the valley of the shadow of death, words become meaningless. The heart oscillates between light and dark and the emotions cannot be trusted. The mind becomes a jumbled mess of chaos and confusion. Darkness surrounds. God's presence is felt only as his absence. No light enters. No feeling sustains. No comfort is found or offered. Not a chosen path, nor a promised destination, the darkness imprisons as a shroud over souls. The words of the prophet are our words: "He has brought me into deep darkness, shutting out all light. He has turned against me. Day and night his hand is heavy upon me...He has buried me in a dark place, like a person long dead" (Lam. 3:2-3, 6 NLT). The valley of the shadow of death is a night of the soul that is beyond the reach of mere words to describe. It is a walk on the edge of the darkest abyss. Some walk there and never return. Some who walked this dark road have survived, but only as those spiritually dead; belief in the goodness of God and hope that his light would once again shine within the soul was destroyed by the numbing darkness. In these moments, night pierces the innermost core of our being. The cry of the heart is a song of mourning and lightness of spirit is a mocker.

The Valley of the Shadow of Death

Walking through the valley of the shadow of death is at times the result of human evil. Brutal actions and merciless sins take their toll on the human spirit. When all kindness and dignity disappear from those around it is difficult to sustain belief in the innate goodness of the human soul. For those who worshipped the potential for goodness within, experiencing the brutality that humanity is capable of deals a death blow to a false god. With hope in the one true God, to rescue and to save, the crippling terror is why the God who is love would allow evil. Darkness by its nature blurs the mind's perspective simply because of the absence of light. Humanity scorns the moral goodness of God shutting out his light. Evil continues its reign of terror because Satan, the Destroyer, exists. Evil exists within the human heart because Adam chose to sin. Evil exists because we live in a world fallen from perfection, terrorizing innocence and corrupting goodness and purity.

Where is God in the face of evil? History remembers the oppression of Israel in Egypt. God saw the injustice and sent Moses to deliver, for the Lord heard the cries of his people. Speaking through the burning bush, the Lord told Moses, "Yes, I am aware of their suffering. So I have come to rescue them from the Egyptians and lead them out of Egypt into their own good and spacious land...flowing with milk and honey" (Ex. 3:7-8 NLT). The Lord saw the evil and sent his deliverance through Moses. But the Lord also told Moses of another prophet who would one day be raised up among the Israelites (Deut. 18:17) to deliver his people, the promised prophet, Messiah Jesus.

When Messiah came he came to die for our sins, but also for every sin committed against us. Evil cannot be ignored or suppressed because if it takes root in the human soul it will consume with a bitterness that imprisons for eternity. We can not wait for those who have sinned against us to ask for forgiveness or be brought to justice, for this may never happen. The only relief from evil committed against us is to find atonement for our sins and for the sins of our enemies. Once atonement has been made we no longer need to carry the burden of bitterness or self-inflicted punishment to pay the price for our own sins and to keep alive within us the sins committed against us in the hope that one day justice will be served. The path to true justice is to place the burden of these sins upon Messiah Jesus for he died a brutal death to atone for brutal sins.

We must put our sins and the sins others have committed against us on him. Messiah is our High Priest (Heb. 4:14) and our sacrifice (John 1:29). Once a year, on Yom Kippur, the Day of Atonement, the High Priest of ancient days would offer sacrifices, first, to atone for his own sins and then for the sins of all Israel. Just as he transferred the sins of all Israel to the sacrifice on the Day of Atonement so Messiah Jesus made atonement for the sins of the whole world (1 John 2:2). Atonement enables forgiveness, but only through the shedding of the blood of the sacrifice accepted by God can there be atonement (Lev. 17:11). This does not lead to an absence of justice, for the words of the Lord are, "I will take revenge; I will pay them back" (Deut. 32:35; Rom. 12:19 NLT), but with atonement the burden of personal justice no longer remains our responsibility; God rises to defend the oppressed.

Bitterness is a burden that allows the oppressor to continue their oppression from thousands of miles away or even from the grave. But true justice is served when the oppressed pray God's blessing upon their enemies and return vengeance into the hands of the Almighty God. It is the Lord's will that justice be served (Gen. 9:5-7) and he has appointed the governing authorities "for the very purpose of punishing those who do what is wrong" (Rom. 13:4 NLT), but when governments fail justice will not fail for in the end the Lord will open "the Book of Life" and all will be "judged according to what they [have] done, as recorded in the books" (Rev. 20:12 NLT). Forgiveness and justice are held together in the hands of God, like grace and truth, and reflect the fullness of the glory of his character. Justice at times is beyond our reach, but forgiveness, an act of goodness in and of itself, is there to be given and received, and is the beginning of the path to freedom from the valley of the shadow of death caused by human evil.

Darkness and Light

"Anyone who is destined for prison will be taken to prison. Anyone destined to die by the sword will die by the sword. This means that God's holy people must endure persecution and remain faithful" (Rev. 13:10 NLT). Strange words to offer those who were suffering in a world hostile to their faith; emperors throwing them to the lions for believing

Jesus is the Messiah. But the comfort in these words is found deeper, below the surface. Who is it that controls our destinies, not just as individuals, but over the entire world? The atheist will say chance. The agnostic will say it can't be known. The believer will say God. And this is the word of comfort: endure for God is in control. If you find yourself in a prison for the sake of righteousness, then know at just the right time the Lord will set you free. If you are suffering, he will bring it to an end. And if it is death you must face, he will raise you to life. Every act of faith in God in the midst of suffering, whether small or great, is itself a defeat of evil.

But if evil inflicts his wounds, is it because he is stronger than God? "And the beast was allowed to wage war against God's holy people and to conquer them" (Rev. 13:7 NLT). God allows suffering, but never the absence of justice. Corrupt leaders, those who followed them, and those who failed to defy their destruction of the innocent, their tyranny over the righteous, their legislation of immorality, will be brought to justice: "they are the ones whose names were not written in the Book of Life before the world was made" (Rev. 13:8 NLT). Known by their actions, but eternally condemned before their life began? Judgment. Sorrow. Darkness.

Light. One Shabbat morning thousands of years ago, under a clear blue Mediterranean sky, Jesus went to synagogue in Natzeret as he had always done (Luke 4:16-28). But on this particular morning, he rose and went to the front to read. At the Bema he was given the scroll of the prophet Isaiah selected for him by the elders from the scrolls of the Hebrew Scriptures. He unrolled the scroll and quoted from these words:

"The Spirit of the Sovereign LORD is on me, because the LORD has anointed me to preach good news to the poor. He has sent me to bind up the brokenhearted, to proclaim freedom for the captives and release from darkness for the prisoners, To proclaim the year of the LORD's favor." (Is. 61:1-2 NIV)

And after he had finished reading, he proclaimed to those who knew him from childhood that, "Today this Scripture is fulfilled in your hearing" (Luke 4:21 NIV). His proclamation of good news was the beginning of the fulfillment of the purpose of his coming to earth as the Mashiach, the promised Messiah, and it continues today. Messiah Jesus came to bring light into our lives. He taught us that, "I have come as a light to shine in this dark world, so that all who put their trust in me will no longer remain in the darkness" (John 12:46 NLT). To those who still dwell in the darkness of the valley of the shadow of death and evil, in Messiah Jesus, we find the light of redemption, Messiah's hope is offered to all, freedom, and the year of the Lord's favor.

Main thought:	Forgiveness is the beginning of the path to freedom from the valley of the shadow of death caused by human evil, but without atonement for sins there can be no real forgiveness.
Key Verse:	"I have come as a light to shine in this dark world, so that all who put their trust in me will no longer remain in the darkness" (John 12:46 NLT).
Question:	Does forgiveness equal the absence of justice?

Chapter Ten

Patience

"Jesus said, 'Here on earth you will have many trials and sorrows. But take heart, because I have overcome the world.'"

John 16:33 [NLT]

Chapter Ten

Patience

Patience is a virtue, so the saying goes, but of all the virtues it is one we have to learn by necessity through desire. A wise mentor once said never to pray for patience for the Lord will answer by making you wait. Wise words taken to heart, but the essence of faith is asking the Lord to provide and waiting for his answer. Even if we embrace wisdom and her words, we must learn to wait while we walk the path of ascent to righteousness.

The Law, the Writings, the Prophets, and the New Testament are filled with the command to wait for the Lord's help and provision, but from an unbeliever's perspective, we who wait on the Lord are naïve fools expecting an unseen God to answer and actually provide for us in a world that we experience through our five senses; the faithful learn to live with this tension. The testing ground of patience reveals it as a virtue that finds its place within the soul at times with peace, at times with a numbness that gnaws at the core of our being. Patience is put to the test when we stand at the crossroads between belief and unbelief, between trusting in God or giving into instant gratification. As at all times, when we choose to trust God we will walk a lonely path for, "the gateway to life is very narrow and the road is difficult, and only a few ever find it" (Matt. 7:14 NLT), but God's promise is that when we do "seek the Kingdom of God above all else, and live righteously he will give [us] everything [we] need" (Matt. 6:33 NLT).

This begs the question, what about the times when it seems that God doesn't provide everything we need. The Scriptures are filled with stories of those who trusted God, but suffered in the absence of the Lord's provision. Abraham was a righteous man and the Lord even called him my friend (Is. 41:8; cf. Jam. 2:23), but his suffering was great. Was the difficult life that Abraham lived the cost of friendship with God or the result? The Scriptures never tell us; most likely it was both.

God promised to make Abraham a great nation, but it wasn't until Abraham was 100 years old that the promised son was born, Isaac born to Sarah (Gen. 21:5). The depth of Abraham's faith was pushed to the edge not long after the promised son was born, when God told Abraham to offer him up as a burnt sacrifice (Gen. 22). We never read of Abraham's incredulity or bitterness, but only of his obedience. We have the advantage of knowing this test of Abraham's faith was not because the Lord wanted Isaac to be sacrificed, Abraham believed in God's provision, but his faith didn't become sight until he passed the test. Abraham never saw the great nation that God promised him, not because of some sin in Abraham's life, but because this was the will of God. Yet still, Abraham believed God and the rest is...well you know. We have the advantage of seeing Abraham's life from beginning to end, while he only saw it one step at a time. It is humbling to make the comparison between his faith and ours, but comparison is not the point. It is God's fulfillment of his promises to Abraham that is meant to strengthen us in whatever situation we find ourselves.

There are a few life-long prayers in my life that still remain unanswered. I'm hoping that the Lord doesn't make me wait until I am 100 like Abraham to have my first son, but I'm still searching for Sarah. There have been unbelievers around me who didn't hide their enjoyment of the fact that God hasn't answered my prayers for a wife. To them it was proof that my belief in God was useless and at times they made sure to rub it in whenever they got the chance; God have mercy on their souls. But there are also those who claim to be believers that have used my unanswered prayers to try and break me.

One especially brutal example happened when I was in the process of joining a small church. At the time I was under the delusion that I should try and become a pastor since I have a Master of Divinity degree, the degree most pastors have. I had asked the leadership of this church to meet with me and give me some advice about how to go about doing this. After waiting for a few weeks they told me that they would meet with me on one particular weeknight. In preparation, I sent them my resume so they could get to know me, although I'd never made a resume for a church before, and at their request wrote out a list of my strengths and weaknesses, and also asked one of my friends to give me her perspective on the same. I put on a jacket and tie out of respect and drove to the church.

Experiencing one of those occasional prophetic inclinations, upon arrival I immediately sensed an eerie mood;

I should've trusted the inclination. I waited for a while until their meeting ended and then they told me to wait in the hall until they were ready for me; something just didn't seem right.

I was led into a small room where the ruling elder, an administrative pastor, and another elder were waiting; the looks on their faces were less than encouraging. I can't remember verbatim the first words they said to me. But the alarm bells went off as soon as this elder said that some of what they were going to say would be "outright rebuke" and that they wouldn't be surprised if I got up and "bolted out of the room." I'd only been going to the church for a few months and this particular elder had never even met me before. I thought they were going to give me some advice and encouragement, maybe even suggest a church I could get involved in, but what took place was more like the Spanish Inquisition. The spirit that filled the room was not grace, but hatred and anger. I remember looking down at the floor and then at the papers I'd prepared for them as he continued to go on and on, and my vision became blurred by tears. For the next hour and a half or so I didn't say much as tears streamed down my face, more out of disbelief and shock than hurt.

This elder said I was being rebuked because I questioned the validity of the 10 percent tithe at a church membership class. He said that the reason the Lord had never answered my prayers was because of my "secret sins" that the Lord had revealed to him because he was the elder of the church, although he never actually told me what these alleged secret sins were (typical modus operandi of Satan). He said that the reason the Lord had never answered my prayers was because of the "sin of my family," although he never explained what that meant. He actually said that, "being single must really suck" (those exact words). He challenged my desire to marry a woman of virtue and actually told me to marry a woman who wasn't even a virgin. He said they were doing me a favor for rebuking me and that in 15 years I would thank them. Then after he was finished he smugly told me he had to go sign a business into bankruptcy (his day job, not a lawyer though). Then they all got up and left me weeping alone in the room.

I told this only because that experience nearly pushed me over the edge. For a few days afterward I was in a daze. I took off school to go snowboarding with a friend to try and get back to reality. I had to choose what I knew was true about myself in the Lord's eyes or accept what they had said. I asked an objective third-party pastor for his input and on his advice I shook the dust off my feet and never went back to that church again. I tried to initiate reconciliation, as per Matt. 18:15-19, but they never responded, maybe one day they will. I wish I could say it was a cult or a fringe group, but it was not. It was a church plant of one of America's "mega-churches."

Truth be told that wasn't the first time I'd experienced the unexpected from Christian leaders. One of those providential ironies was that this kind of treatment began soon after my parents divorced when I was 17, but this was a whole new level of brutality. There is some comfort in thinking that all of this happened for a greater purpose, for some grand plan that will one day explain it all, but the reality is that the Lord has not decreed that everyone go from prison to Pharaoh's palace. Seeking the Lord's face and asking him to make you into a righteous man demands payment of the high price of suffering, but if we share in his suffering we will share in his glory (Rom. 8:17). But true faith is not giving up the hope of love and the blessings of the Lord in this life in exchange for future glory. It is precisely the opposite. It is never giving up hope and each day expecting the Lord's blessings in this life, and in the life to come, for God gives good gifts to his children (Matt. 7:11).

I offer my prayers to the Lord and I believe he will answer in his time. This is the testing ground of patience. Some may think it naïve to believe that God will actually answer my prayers for a godly wife who loves Messiah Jesus with all her heart, soul, mind, and strength. A woman who does her husband [moral] good and not [moral] evil all the days of her life (Prov. 31:12), from the moment she was born to the moment we die, consciously living a life of sexual purity so that she can present herself to me pure on our wedding night, a woman who is an Eshet-Chayil (wife of virtue). But I do trust God and I will never compromise God's Law and promises. With all due respect, look where Abraham's compromise got us.

Everyone only gets one first time and God's intention was for a man and woman, husband and wife, to experience their first time with each other on their wedding night. To fill their lifetime with the mystery of anticipation and romance, pleasure and intimacy, the passion and the beauty of sex, and to create an unbreakable physical, emotional, and spiritual bond of love for each other to the exclusion of all others. God's intention for marriage was for the covenant of marriage to be between, one man and one woman, husband and wife, for their entire lives. He even provided a physical sign to mark the beginning of the marriage covenant. As with most of the covenants the Lord God made with man throughout human history, he intended marriage to be entered into through blood and this is why he designed the male and female anatomy the way he did (Deut. 22:13-21). It may not sound romantic, but it is reality. Just as God's covenant with Abraham is entered through blood by the unbroken continuity of circumcision as a sign of membership in the covenant family of Israel to this day, so it is God's intention and design for entering into the covenant of marriage and the beginning of a new family. God created sex, but he created it for marriage.

Anyone who doubts that God's intention is for both men and women to not engage in sex until marriage need only read God's commandments regarding sexual purity found all throughout the Law. One section is found in Deut. 22:13-30. Here you find what was to be done with a woman discovered to be sleeping around while she lived in her father's home (Deut. 22:20-21). This passage is about a woman who is unmarried for a woman would only leave her father's home when she married. The consequence of promiscuity was severe, death. The same is true of men. The Law makes no allowance for casual sex. If a man had sex with a woman who was engaged to be married in a context where no one witnessed what took place (in the country side), the Law doesn't even call it promiscuity, it calls this man's actions rape. In this context only the man was to be killed as the Law assumes the innocence and virtue of the woman (Deut. 22:25). But if it was in a context where others could have heard (a town) then both were to be killed because she did not scream for help (Deut. 22:24). If she was a virgin and not engaged, then the young man had to marry her (and pay her father 50 pieces of silver), because he took away her purity, and he was never allowed to divorce her (Deut. 22:28-29). The point is that in the eyes of the Lord, sexual promiscuity and immorality has severe consequences and is deserving of death; "the wages of sin is death" (Rom. 6:23 NLT). If this is how the Lord looks upon what society considers "casual sex" how much more so does the Lord hate adultery, which destroys the sacred covenant of marriage (Ex. 20:14), and even more so, the vile abomination of sexual perversion (Lev. 18:22; 20:13) upon which he rained down fire from heaven (Gen. 19:1-29) to make them an example of the coming judgment (2 Pet. 2:6). Regardless of what one believes about the Law it expresses God's mind, will, and deep hatred for sin with specific application to specific sins.

In response, I've heard some say, "but God told Hosea to marry a prostitute." To be honest, I've only ever heard this from women. I have compassion for those who feel the deep wound left by the absence of sexual purity, for the Lord has written this on every heart. But still, maybe I've never fully understood their objection or maybe I have. Hosea's wife was a prostitute and God did command Hosea to marry her. But do these women want their husbands to think of them as prostitutes? A woman's mind is complex, but could part of the answer be, yes? The very reason Hosea was commanded to marry a prostitute was so that his actions would be a sign to Israel that even though she, Israel, had prostituted herself to the false gods of the Ancient Near East the Lord's love for Israel would never cease, that God's promise to Abraham would continue: "I will bless those who bless you and curse those who treat you with contempt. *All the families of the earth will be blessed through you*" (Gen. 12:3 NLT). God still loved Israel even though she had sinned against him. Perhaps, this is what these women are pointing to: forgiveness. They don't want to lose hope that they will one day find a man who will deeply love them and want to be their husband even though they've made mistakes. Maybe a woman who would raise this does think of herself as a prostitute because she knows that she has destroyed the most sacred, precious, and honoring gift that she could give to her husband, and that gift is herself. Maybe what she seeks is a man to love her so that she would feel forgiven for her sins. But that is the wrong reason for marriage.

Forgiveness for our sins can only come from one place for only the Lord God can forgive sins. No man can carry the burden of his wife's sins, nor can she carry his, though some try, they will always fail. Those who marry to become messiahs end up with a lifetime of crucifixion. The place to atone for our sins is at the feet of Jesus. Remember the prostitute who humbled herself and wept at the feet of Jesus. And Jesus said, "I tell you, her sins and they are many have been forgiven, so she has shown me much love. But a person who is forgiven little shows only little love. Then Jesus said to the woman, Your sins are forgiven" (Luke 7:47 NLT). This is the place to find forgiveness. And in the mystery of the goodness of God, through humility and forgiveness, our sins are transformed into a deep love for God, a love that is expressed through righteousness (Ps. 130:3-4).

Marriage requires a lifetime of forgiveness for it is always entered into by a man and a woman who are sinful, but forgiveness should not be the reason for marriage. Marriage should be that potent mix of the chemistry and excitement of attraction, compatibility in heart, mind and soul, and the electrifying difference of male and female, the two becoming one flesh, strength and beauty. Seeking a partner for life requires first a complete and total honest look at oneself. When God made Eve for Adam he made her to be a perfect fit with Adam, to be his companion and helper in the task that God had created Adam to carryout. In the same way, it is a man's responsibility to know who he is and what his purpose is in this life and then seek out and pursue a woman who is as perfect a fit as possible with him and his calling. He should be realistic with who he is and then embark out into the world to seek and pursue his match created for him by the Creator. This naturally begins with her physical appearance, but includes all other areas such as personality, moral character, spirituality, intelligence, humor, passion, and purpose. If a man marries a woman whom he considers less than his equal in worth she will never feel truly loved, and as a result he will never be truly respected. But when a man marries a woman he considers equal in worth to him, mysteriously different but matched and suitable for him, the result will be that he will never feel worthy of her for it will be easy to love her and her response of love and respect will always be a mystery; Adam and Eve.

The problem today is not unrealistic comparison and expectations because of images in the media, but a failure to know ourselves and set our expectations of our potential husband or wife by the standard of who we actually are in reality. Even more so, our generation has forsaken seeking the Lord's face to pray and fast for a godly spouse, and then put our faith into action by living lives of integrity and righteousness, and waiting for the Lord to lead and provide.

The blessing from the Lord that the righteous man is promised is a wife who brings pleasure into his home like a fruitful vine along with wisdom, understanding, and respect (Ps. 128; Prov. 19:14), and the love and intimacy that a woman seeks is lavished upon the woman who fears the Lord (Prov. 31:30).

I will be the first to say that following the wisdom of God is difficult and as I write I still live with the hope of love that is still just hope and prayers. I underestimated the price I would have to pay to wait for the Lord's answer to my prayers for an Eshet-Chayil, but this is the path of wisdom that I chose and her price is costly, far above rubies (Prov. 31:10). No compromise means putting faith into action and covenanting before the Lord with all our soul and all our strength to not engage in sexual immorality and to not even look lustfully at a woman or her image (Matt. 5:28). Giving up is for losers and the weak and not one of the characteristics of those who follow after Messiah Jesus, and not the ambition of those who run the race of faith to win. We must never forget Paul's words: "so let's not get tired of doing what is good. At just the right time we will reap a harvest of blessing if we don't give up" (Gal. 6:9 NLT). Blessings are a gift from God, but patience is a virtue.

Chapter Eleven

Faith in the Midst of Suffering

"I have refined you but not as silver is refined. Rather, I have refined you in the furnace of suffering."

Isaiah 48:10 [NLT]

Chapter Eleven

Faith in the Midst of Suffering

Finding faith in the midst of suffering is difficult. Walking through times of suffering surrounded by confusion and the disconnected reality it brings, one is haunted by the accusation that our suffering is punishment from God; that our faith is offered in vain. The challenge to faith arises not from the pain or grief or sadness we experience, but from the doubts about whether we are truly loved by God. Abstract discussions about the problem of evil that question the goodness or sovereignty of God are a fallen faith's reasoning; childish and shallow. For the believer there is never any question about the goodness of God. The question that pierces the soul is why God's goodness is absent from our lives. This is the cry of, "my God, my God, why have you forsaken me" (Ps. 22:1; Matt. 27:46 NIV). Those who have known this cry have walked through the "furnace of suffering" (Is. 48:10). Those who have come through humbled and stronger in faith are the privileged children of God. For those who have fallen in their trial, grace remains.

The Origin of Suffering

There was a time when suffering did not exist. The perfection of Eden was a garden without pain. In absolute purity, Adam and his wife Eve dwelt in love and intimacy with one another and with God. The Scriptures present a world that began in perfection. God pronounced his blessing of goodness on everything he made. The pinnacle of his creation was humanity, Adam and Eve, man and woman, created to unite and become one flesh in body and soul, made in the image of God. "And God looked over all that he had made, and he saw that it was very good" (Gen. 1:31 NLT). God's creation was an expression of his sovereign power to create and his fundamental goodness that is a part of everything he created. In the midst of the garden God had planted a tree, the tree of the knowledge of good and evil, and God had forbidden Adam and Eve to eat of the tree. The consequence of eating of the fruit of that tree was death. This death was not just the end of life, but the entry of evil into the world.

Tragically, Adam and Eve ate of the forbidden tree and all of humanity was condemned to die. Adam's failure was the result of choosing evil and allowing the serpent's lies to take root. It was the serpent, Satan the Accuser, who tricked Eve and it was Eve's deception that blurred the resolution of Adam's will to obey God. As a result of Adam's rebellion our first ancestors were banished from paradise and from that moment on human existence became a life of trials, suffering, and pain. Suffering has always seemed wrong for the memory of Eden and a longing to return there has remained deep within the human soul. The images we see of white sandy beaches and tropical palms, golden sunsets and lovers embracing, offers the hope of a momentary return to paradise without evil, but in the reality of our days we only know of goodness shrouded with the thorns of suffering, and the deceptive accusations of the serpent. We live outside of paradise. We live in a fallen world.

God is sovereign over suffering

Suffering is universally experienced by humanity and at times we are tempted to doubt either the goodness of God or his sovereignty. When theologians write of the sovereignty of God they are writing of God's unlimited power and total control over everything that happens. God is the highest authority in the universe. He is the King above all other kings and the Lord above all other rulers. There is nothing that happens in the universe that is outside of his control, including suffering.

Suffering is the theme central to the wisdom literature of the Scriptures as recorded in the Book of Job. In these ancient words there is no gloss over the depth of pain that Job experienced, nor a condemnation of his anguish. Rather, through the darkness of human suffering the goodness of the character of God and his sovereignty over his creation is revealed and reaffirmed.

Pulling back the veil that separates us from the kingly Court of Heaven, we read in the first chapter of the book of Job that Satan, the Accuser (in Hebrew 'satan' literally means 'accuser' or 'adversary') approached God along with the others in the court of heaven. Satan had been watching humanity from a distance, and "patrolling the earth" (Job 1:7 NLT). And the Lord asked Satan if he had noticed Job. The Lord deeply loved and respected Job and told Satan, "He is the finest man in all the earth. He is blameless – a man of complete integrity. He fears God and stays away from evil" (Job 1:8 NLT). In God's eyes, Job was a good and righteous man; God deeply loved Job.

In accord with his nature, full of bitterness and jealousy, Satan immediately attacked the Lord's love for Job and Job's integrity and love for God. Satan brought this accusation: "Job has good reason to fear God...you have made him prosper in everything he does. Look how rich he is...take away everything he has, and he will surely curse you to your face" (Job 1:10-11 NLT). Satan viewed Job's righteousness as the shallow response to material prosperity and blessing from God, that God was an infinite, divine manipulator tricking humanity into loving him by trading material prosperity in exchange for their devotion and worship. As far as Satan was concerned the only reason Job loved God was because Job was selfish, not righteous, and so was God. God gave Job what he wanted so God could get what he wanted – to be worshipped by Job. Even more, Satan's accusation was not just against Job, Satan attacked the loving kindness and goodness of God that irresistibly drew the righteous to the Lord to love and worship him. Satan hated God and Job.

Satan's accusation reflected his true nature. Satan's hatred for God and the righteous was fueled by his own bitterness and evil (Rev. 12:7-18). Once an angel in Heaven,

Satan had risen up against God in an attempt to set himself up in the Heavenly Temple of God to be worshipped as God. He gathered to himself many among the angels in heaven to fight and try to overthrow God and the Armies of Heaven. In his foolish campaign, Satan was defeated and cast down to the earth with all the angels who followed him, and on the earth, he established his kingdom of darkness. He set up false religions to deceive humanity into worshipping him, with the intent to destroy everything God made to be good, and imprison humanity in darkness away from God. Satan offered temporary material blessing and prosperity, success and power, in exchange for their worship (Luke 4:6-7). Thus, Satan brought his accusation to prove that he was just like God. Take away material blessing and prosperity, success and power, and Job would turn against God because he would no longer have any reason to worship him, and Job's love for God would be exactly the same as those on the earth that bowed and worshipped Satan.

And if Job did curse God and turn against him, Satan would be vindicated for his defeat in heaven. It would be proven that he was just as powerful as God for he produced the same kind of worship in humanity, as God had produced in Job. Inflict suffering upon Job and blame it on God as punishment for unrighteousness, and his faith would crumple and Job's love for God and belief in God's goodness would be destroyed, once and for all. And through defeating Job, whom God deeply loved, Satan would defeat the Lord God.

But if Job did not curse God but remained devoted to him, the depth of Job's love for God and faith in God's loving kindness and goodness would be a vindication of the reality of the goodness of God's character, and a love that was so strong that even when Job did not understand the reason or cause of his suffering, he would still remain faithful and devoted to God. It would prove that Job loved God because of who God was and not because of prosperity and riches. Through Job's suffering the Lord would reaffirm that he "does not enjoy hurting people or causing them sorrow" (Lam. 3:33 NLT), but that in this world there comes a time when suffering must be endured to defeat evil. The Lord chose Job for this task because among all those on the earth, he was most favored and deeply loved by the Lord. The Lord knew that Job would never give up for the knowledge of the goodness of God was deeply planted in Job's heart like the beauty of creation in the Garden of Eden. Job was given a messianic calling, even though he was not aware of it. He was called to endure through suffering with the hope that he would once again see the goodness of the Lord, and by so doing overcome his unseen adversary, Satan, and the evil he inflicted. Job's faithful endurance would give hope to the faithful on the earth so that they, in turn, would also persevere and overcome evil, and declare that the Lord God alone is God, Creator of the Heavens and the Earth, sovereign over the universe.

Thus, the Court of Heaven was in session as God allowed Job to be tested, and he himself, allowed the goodness of his own character to be put on trial. Satan began his arguments and unleashed suffering upon Job.

We know that Job suffered greatly. His very own wife taunted him to "curse God and die" (Job 2:9) as she succumbed to the unseen deception of Satan. Job refused and affirmed that God was sovereign over both good and evil (Job 2:8-10). When

Job's friends first arrived their empathy for the depth of his suffering was expressed with silence. Then Job spoke.

Job maintained that he was a righteous man and his insistence on his own innocence provoked his friends to challenge Job and question his integrity. Job had lost his sons and daughters and possessions and now he was betrayed by his own friends. Job fell into a deep depression and questioned why he was born and even longed for death (Job 9:18-22). Yet Job never cursed God and never gave up belief in God's ultimate goodness; "though he slay me, yet will I hope in him" (Job 13:15 NIV). Job maintained his innocence to the end. Then the Lord spoke.

Out of a whirlwind the Lord challenged Job. Not with a rebuke for sin or self-righteousness as some suggest, but with the words, "brace yourself like a man" (Job 38:3; 40:7 NIV). Job had suffered greatly but the words the Lord spoke to him were not gentle words of compassion, but strong words intended to restore Job as a man among men. All the words of the Lord spoken to Job were a declaration of the Lord's strength and absolute sovereignty as Creator over his creation (Job 38-41). Job had to face the truth as a man that everything that had happened to him was under the control of God, even though God's purpose for the suffering he endured was never revealed to him. When Job eventually received consolation from his family and friends, the writer of Job, wanting to make sure that we, the readers, didn't miss the point, included that Job suffered and was now comforted "because of all the trials the Lord had brought against him" (Job 42:11 NLT). There can be no dispute that Job's suffering was from the Lord, but remember that God deeply loved Job. God is sovereign over suffering. In allowing Job to be tested God had risked belief in his own goodness. God had risked losing Job's devotion as his own innocent children were tragically slaughtered by Satan. But the Lord knew that his own eternal goodness would overcome for his goodness is indisputably evident as "the Heavens declare the glory of God" (Ps. 19:1 KJV) and that his goodness was undeniably ingrained deep into Job's heart; the Lord was confident that his goodness would overcome the deepest of Job's suffering, even though the pain of suffering was great.

And God's goodness did overcome. Job never cursed God. God's goodness was vindicated and in the High Court of Heaven it was declared that the Lord alone is God. It was established that Job's love for God was not because of the material blessings that God gave him, but because of who God is, his goodness and loving kindness, even in the face of suffering. The wisdom of the Book of Job teaches us that the suffering of the righteous, when no reason or purpose is seen or known, is not a result of their sin; it is not punishment from God. The love of the righteous for God is a deep love that overcomes the darkest of evil and the most bitter of enemies, and endures. Every act of faith in the midst of suffering, no matter how small or great, declares a victory over evil, and is an act of love for God. There is a mystery and power to this love, and when it is known, it is a glory filled with the beauty of the Lord like his glory that is displayed in the heavens. The depth of God's love for Job and Job's devotion to God overcame the suffering that had to be endured for a time and for a purpose.

Upon completion of the testing, the Lord unconditionally restored his blessing upon Job's life. The Lord brought justice to those who had treated Job with contempt. God commanded Job's false friends to repent for they had spoken falsely about God and the reason he allowed Job to suffer, unlike the words Job had spoken about God (Job 42:7). God commanded them to ask Job to pray for them and offer sacrifices to atone for their sins so that they would be forgiven by the Lord (Job 42:8). And Job prayed for his friends. After justice was served upon Job's false comforters, the Lord restored his blessing upon Job with feasting and celebration so that Job could say "thou preparest a table before me in the presence of mine enemies" (Ps. 23:5 KJV) and "I have been young, and now am old; yet I have not seen the righteous forsaken" (Ps. 37:25 KJV). In fact, the Lord blessed Job more after his trial of suffering than he had before (Job 42:12). Job suffered, but he endured and never gave up his belief and trust in the Lord even though everything was taken away from him; his deep faith was a result of his deep knowledge of God's character. In the end, Satan was silenced and defeated in the court of Heaven. God's goodness was established without dispute. For those who love the Lord, love him because he is good.

God's redemption through suffering

But the problem of suffering does not end with the story of Job. In the Lord's eyes suffering is wrong and in violation of his goodness. The Lord in his eternal wisdom had in place a strategy to defeat Satan and suffering and redeem humanity and all of creation from evil, a strategy formulated from before the foundations of the world (Rev. 13:8). Evil entered the world through Adam's sin and brought death into the world that "spread to everyone" and "everyone sinned" (Rom. 5:12 NLT); after Adam, evil reigned over the earth.

The defeat of evil could take place if a second Adam would arise who like Adam was perfect and without sin and who would choose to obey God. This second Adam would be the savior of all humanity – a Messiah – who by his endurance through suffering like Job, and obedience to the purpose of God, would lead the way to a world filled with goodness and a return to the perfection of the Garden of Eden. The obstacle facing the second Adam would be the removal of the unavoidable consequences of the sin of Adam and the criminal acts of his descendants, humanity. In the Court of Heaven, the violation of Eternal Law was charged against humanity by Satan the Accuser and there would be no return to Eden without punishment for the crimes of humanity. Humanity's criminal acts were brutal and the punishment for such brutality was death; paradise regained without due rendering of punishment would be a violation of Eternal justice fundamental to the goodness and consistency of the character of God.

For this reason the second Adam would be required to not only choose to obey where Adam had chosen to rebel, but he would be required to suffer to remove the criminal charges against humanity. In the Court of Heaven there can be no plea bargaining or acquittal. Satan had made his case and the punishment for the charges against humanity was eternal death. An absence of punishment would be the absence of justice. The only way for the second Adam to lead the way to paradise would be to satisfy the justice of the Court and this is precisely what he did.

The second Adam is Messiah Jesus

The second Adam is Messiah Jesus. This is not a new or novel idea, but tried and tested truth taken directly out of the Scriptures. It was Adam's sin that brought condemnation upon us all, but Messiah's "one act of righteousness makes all people right in God's sight and gives them life" (Rom 5:18 NLT). Death is synonymous with evil; life is synonymous with paradise without evil. Life is the legal right to once again be children of God like Adam and enjoy the close intimacy he had with God and one day dwell in the new Garden of Eden – the new Heavens and the new Earth (Rev. 21). We know according to the Scriptures that Jesus led a perfect life (Is. 53:9; 2 Cor. 5:21) and like Adam before the fall was a sinless man. In this, Jesus was unique among all born from woman. His moral perfection gave him the privilege to be in a position to make the choice of the second Adam and vindicate Adam and all humanity by choosing to obey God.

The reason Jesus was given the right to be the second Adam is because of the goodness of God. In the Court of Heaven, God is the presiding judge. Providing a Messiah was the will of God to do away with evil once and for all and do so in a manner that fully satisfied Justice. However, the choice that faced Jesus was infinitely more difficult than the one that faced Adam. Adam had only to refrain from eating of the fruit of one particular tree in a garden full of fruit-bearing trees in a world without evil and suffering. The second Adam had to make his choice in the context of a fallen world full of evil and suffering weighing upon his shoulders. He had to not only make a choice, but to also satisfy the judgment of death handed down against humanity. The choice given him by the Judge of the Court of Heaven was to either choose to take on himself the punishment for the crimes of humanity or to choose to save his own life. The second Adam chose to obey God, his Father, the Judge of the Court of Heaven, and to sacrifice his own life and drink of the cup of suffering to satisfy the punishment due Adam and humanity; to take on himself the penalty for "the sins of the whole world" (1 John 2:2 NIV). And Jesus said, "my Father...not my will, but thine, be done" (Luke 22:42 KJV).

There is no irony in the fact that historically Jesus was condemned to die through legal trial. First, Jesus was tried by the Sanhedrin, the Jewish Supreme Court that administered the affairs of the Jewish people during the period of Roman occupation. The Sanhedrin questioned Jesus directly asking if he was the Messiah. Jesus answered, "You have said it. And in the future you will see the Son of Man seated in the place of power at God's right hand and coming on the clouds of heaven" (Matt. 26:64 NLT). At this answer the High Priest tore his clothes and the Sanhedrin rendered their verdict and falsely found Jesus guilty of blasphemy because he claimed that he himself was equal with God. They condemned him to die since blasphemy carried the penalty of death (Lev. 24:16; Matt. 26:64-66).

The second trial was under Pontius Pilate, the governor presiding over the Roman province of Judea (Israel in the 1st century C.E.). Pilate condemned Jesus to death by crucifixion even though he had found no reason to execute him. Through these human courts the High Court of Heaven placed the punishment rendered against Adam and all humanity upon Messiah Jesus "in accordance with God's predetermined plan" (Acts 2:23 CJB). And Jesus cried out, "my God, my God, why have you forsaken me" (Ps. 22:1; Matt. 27:46 NIV). No mere human could have taken this punishment upon himself for the sins of all humanity crossed the boundaries of space and time; the Suffering Messiah by necessity had to be the divine Son of God. It was because of God's goodness and his love for his people Israel and the nations, that he both offered and accepted the sacrifice of Messiah, to do away with evil and suffering once and for all, and to give passage to the eternal Eden, but only to those who believe (John 3:16).

In the end God will be merciful

Like Joseph in Egypt, Messiah Jesus suffered to save the people of God as Mashiach Ben-Yosef (see chapter 3). The suffering of Jesus by the hands of his brothers was of the same nature that Joseph experienced. Joseph's words are equally true of Jesus when Joseph said, "you intended to harm me, but God intended it all for good. He brought me to this position so I could save the lives of many people" (Gen. 50:19-20 NLT). It is no accident that when God himself took on human flesh to save humanity he came as a "man of sorrows, and acquainted with grief" (Is. 53:3 KJV) for he came to identify with the suffering of his people Israel, and the nations. The world into which Messiah came was a fallen world in which the pinnacle of creation, humanity made in the image of God, suffered greatly. Jesus came to share in our suffering and through his own suffering to redeem us all and lead us into the eternal Eden, a world where "there will be no more death or sorrow or crying or pain" (Rev. 21:4 NLT).

For those who suffer now the word of the Lord is persevere and endure. For just as we read in the story of Job, the "Lord was kind to him at the end, for the Lord is full of tenderness and mercy" (Jms. 5:11 NLT), we too shall see the goodness and salvation of the Lord at his appointed time. Our calling as the children of God is to persevere and endure for in due time we will once again know the "goodness of the Lord in the land of the living" (Ps. 27:13 KJV). Our suffering is not in vain when endured for the sake of Messiah, for if we share in his suffering we will also share in his glory (Rom. 8:17), and every act of faith in God in the midst of suffering is a defeat of evil and darkness. A time of suffering is a privileged gift given to God's beloved children to teach us that the reason we love him is not conditional upon the blessings he gives us, but rather, that we love him because of who he is; God is good.

Main Thought: Suffering is wrong in God's eyes, but it is through the tragedy of suffering that we realize we love the Lord not because of his blessings to us, but because of his character, because he is good. It is because of God's goodness that he provided the Messiah to bring an end to suffering once and for all.

Key Verse: *"I have refined you, but not as silver is refined. Rather, I have refined you in the furnace of suffering."* Isaiah 48:10

Question: Have you experienced a depth of suffering that has challenged your faith in God and has caused you to question God's goodness or his sovereignty?

Chapter Twelve

Boomerang Blessings

"But the Lord reigns forever, executing judgment from his throne. He will judge the word with justice and rule the nations with fairness. The Lord is a shelter for the oppressed, a refuge in times of trouble."

Psalm 9:7-9 [NLT]

Chapter Twelve

Boomerang Blessings

You don't have to dig too deep into the Scriptures to find evidence of this master of all conspiracy theories, the divine conspiracy[1], at work over and over again throughout history, turning the cursing of an enemy into blessings for his chosen. Nebuchadnezzar brought the curse of exile upon Judah in 597 B.C.E. and the destruction of the Temple. But rulers rise and fall and Nebuchadnezzar was soon replaced by Cyrus of the Persians to reign in Saddam's palace. The Lord turned Nebuchadnezzar's curse of destruction into Cyrus' blessing of life anew in the Promised Land as Cyrus sent the exiles back to Judah in 538 B.C.E. While Nebuchadnezzar destroyed the Temple, Cyrus gave orders to rebuild it. Cursing was transformed into blessing.

History repeats itself for the simple reason that for every evil conspiracy that seeks to destroy God's people there is a divine conspiracy to overcome it. Hitler's curse of destruction was defeated by life anew for the Jewish people in the Promised Land by decree of the United Nations in 1948. Return from exile never came without conflict for the simple

---

[1] I borrowed the title from: Dallas Willard, *The Divine Conspiracy*, (San Francisco: Harper, 1998).

reason that rebuilding the Temple was never easy when surrounded by a persistent enemy bent on destruction whether it was 538 B.C.E. or 1948 C.E. (figuratively speaking as far as the Temple goes).

Our spiritual warfare is never against flesh and blood, but the principalities and powers of this dark world (Eph. 6:12), the angels of destruction led by Satan himself. Satan has a persistent weakness that is his perpetual downfall: his pride and disbelief in his own defeat blinds him from seeing the divine conspiracy at work. His deception falls like hypnosis on some and the greatest of all human tragedies is that some fall prey to Satan's mysticism and try to manipulate the darkness to achieve their own ends; this is always foolish for a curse of darkness against the righteous always boomerangs, but not in the way that those who curse might expect.

There once was a man who cursed with violence and who uttered threats with every breath (Acts 9:1) filled with hatred not only did he approve of the killing of those who followed Messiah Jesus, but he himself hunted them down to kill them himself out of what he thought was zeal for God. His name was Shaul, and he was a Rabbi trained as a Pharisee and raised at the feet of Gamaliel. In God's divine goodness and wisdom, he always has a way of turning the most violent of cursing into the most prolific of blessings.

Shaul's cursing boomeranged big time back onto Shaul, but not in the way you might expect. Not only did Shaul stop killing the followers of Messiah Jesus, but he actually became a believer in Jesus himself. God didn't stop there. While before Shaul traveled the world to kill believers, God changed him into the Rabbi of the Gentiles, Paul the Apostle, traveling the world to take the message of Messiah Jesus to all nations and make believers. And to top it all off he didn't put Shaul's rabbinical training and zeal to waste, but the Lord used him so that he became the most prolific writer of the New Covenant Scriptures; the divine conspiracy has a strong foundation of divine irony. But don't miss the point, if the Lord did it once he will do it again, and for some reason, I suspect, sooner rather than later.

From this perspective one can't help but feel sorry for those who curse others with death and failure for they don't realize what they're playing with and they don't know what they're getting themselves into. Messiah died for a reason, and that, to bring an end to all curses so those who curse will fail when they curse his little Mashiachs (Christian means little Messiah, *Mashiach ketan* or *Meshechim ketanim* I guess). But what they don't realize is that their curses will never work on a little Mashiach; they will always boomerang back, but with the blessing of Messiah. Those who cursed yesterday will soon be the very ones proclaiming the Gospel of Messiah to the Nations and being used by the Lord to answer the prayers of the righteous. With the Lord blessing is always disproportional to the cursing. With God a little cursing goes a long way to be transformed into a forest of blessing for the Lord has a knack for taking the insignificant and obscure, say for example, five loaves and two fishes, and using them to feed Israel, with twelve baskets left over just to make sure no one misses the point (Mark 6:43).

And this is always God's point, he is the God who rises to defend the oppressed, the helpless, and the needy; he loves the irony with divine delight. Above all other events in human history it is in the life of Mashiach himself that the divine conspiracy achieved the greatest victory. Satan walked into the trap of his own pride and hatred and he fell in hook, line, and sinker. In the wilderness Satan tempted Jesus and offered him the kingdoms of the world and all their glory if only Messiah would bow to worship him (Matt.4:8-9). At the crucifixion, Satan's pride and delight in the failure of God's Mashiach to establish the messianic Kingdom was exactly what blinded him from the complete and total defeat that was about to fall on his head. As soon as Messiah uttered the words, "It is finished" (John 19:30) Satan thought he won. But he was wrong.

God always turns cursing into blessing for those whom he loves. God raised Messiah from the dead and not only was he given the authority over the kingdoms of this world, God made him "Melech HaOlam," King of the Universe, "that in honor of the name given Yeshua, every knee will bow in heaven, on earth and under the earth and every tongue will acknowledge that Yeshua the Messiah is ADONAI, to the glory of God the Father" (Phil. 2:11 CJB). This is God's natural law: if you try to kill his Mashiach he may let him die for a time and for a purpose, but then he will raise him from the dead and bless him far above what the one who cursed could have ever offered.

The same is true for Messiah's little Mashiachs. These are dark times and they are few and far between in pulpit and pew, but you will find them. You won't hear too many of them on the radio, and even fewer will ever be on CNN, but if you look hard you'll see these little Mashiachs. He will be the young husband who lost his young wife, but decided to write "I still believe" in the midst of his pain. She will be the wife and mother who awakens one morning to find her body wracked with cancer, but pours out her selfless love into her husband and children. He will be the evangelist who tragically lost his son, but devoted his life to mentoring the next generation of leaders. She will be the loving wife and mother who lost her husband and son and daughter in the tragedy of a plane crash, but continued on with the ministry they began together to shine the light of Messiah into a hurting world. He will be the pastor whose illness took him out of the pulpit for months, but who rose again to say, "blessed be the name of Lord."

Many of them will be abandoned and forsaken in spirit by friends and family in their suffering. They will be accused of all kinds of evil by false prophets, even accused of allegiance to the enemy. They will be hated and even scorned as forsaken by God. And this is why the Lord loves them so much and why he waits until just the right time to pour out his blessing and favor.

The Lord waits until their enemies think they have finished and succeeded in their conspiracy of evil, their forced exile and destruction, their crucifixion of the righteous, and then God moves swiftly to justice. For the little Mashiachs crucifixion always comes first just as it did with Messiah, but then at just the right time, to bring the greatest blessing to his dearly loved child, and to bring the greatest glory to His name, resurrection takes place and overcomes evil to the amazement of those who love him.

This is God's natural law. The very thing that the enemies cursed against the righteous to prevent and destroy the desire of their hearts, the Lord takes and transforms into a masterpiece of blessing for his deeply loved children.

The divine conspiracy is always at work and just when it seems that all hope is lost he unveils his glory so that it shines like the brightness of the noonday sun and refreshes their soul like the crispness and beauty of the morning sky (Ps. 37:6). God's blessing erases the memory of the darkest curse and surrounds his little Mashiach with his goodness, love, and righteousness.

Conclusion

God is unseen, but there will come a time when our faith will become sight and the entire sum of human history will be a parenthesis between Adam walking with God in the Garden of Eden and the New Jerusalem (Rev. 21) filled with the glorious presence of God. In this present life, the Lord will give us reminders of his love and goodness, a loving wife or husband, children, family, a satisfying career. He reminds us of his goodness when we see an awe-inspiring sunset or appreciate the wonder of his creation. We encounter hardship and suffering, but when it is overcome it causes us to appreciate the good things he has given us more deeply. In all this, as we walk through this life, we walk by faith not by sight. But we can be sure that one day we will use our senses to know God in a way that we don't in this present life. The Scriptures remind us to fix our eyes on what is unseen and what is eternal (2 Cor. 4:18), but one day faith will become sight. Our understanding and knowledge of God in this world is like seeing things "imperfectly as in a poor mirror," but one day "we will see everything with perfect clarity" and "know everything completely, just as God knows" us now (1 Cor. 13:12 NLT).

The destiny for those who believe is eternal life lived in an eternal body where everything is experienced through the five senses. A body just like the one Messiah Jesus received when he rose from the dead. It is no coincidence that he is called the "first fruits" of all who have died (1 Cor. 15:20 NLT) for in his human nature he was the first to receive the eternal body that all those who believe in him will receive. And united with his divine nature he ascended to the Father's right hand of power. The hope for seeing God in our human body is among the most ancient known to man as expressed by the words of Job:

"But as for me, I know that my Redeemer lives, and that he will stand upon the earth at last. And after my body has decayed, yet in my body I will see God! I will see him for myself. Yes, I will see him with my own eyes. I am overwhelmed at the thought!" (Job 19:25-27 NLT)

The faithful live between two worlds, this world and the Kingdom of God, where the light of the glory of God and the Lamb of God fill the City of God, the New Jerusalem, with the divine presence (Rev. 21:23), and will once again eat "from the tree of life in the paradise of God" (Rev. 2:7 NLT). The Sh'kinah that filled the most Holy Place in the ancient temple in Jerusalem will fill the whole the City of God with his glory (Rev. 21:22) so that there will be no need for any other source of light (Rev. 21:23).

Those who do not believe will also see God in their flesh, but suffer for eternity with the knowledge that they rejected him in their lives on earth. The conclusion is that either way, believing or unbelieving, we shall all see God. The humble King is the returning King, and his word is the final word:

"See, I am coming soon, and my reward is with me, to repay all according to their deeds. I am the Alpha and the Omega, the First and the Last, the Beginning and the End" (Rev.22:12 NLT).

Appendix I

    The following is a list of passages from the Tanakh (Old Testament) that were considered to be about the Messiah in ancient rabbinic writings as compiled by Alfred Edersheim.[1] English translation numbering is indicated. Hebrew numbering is in brackets.

Genesis	1:2; 2:4; 3:15; 4:25; 8:11; 9:27; 14:1; 18:4; 19:32; 22:18; 33:1; 49:1; 49:9; 49:10; 49:12; 49:17; 49:19; 50:10.
Exodus	4:22; 12:2; 12:42; 15:1; 16:25; 16:33; 17:16; 21:1; 40:9,11.
Leviticus	26:13.
Numbers	6:26; 7:12; 11:26; 23:21; 24:17; 24:17; 27:16.
Deuteronomy	1:8; 11:21; 16:3; 19:8,9; 20:10; 23:11; 25:19; 32:7; 32:30; 33:5; 33:12; 33:17.
Judges	5:31.
Ruth	1:1; 2:14; 3:15; 4:18.
1 Samuel	2:10.

---

[1] For complete list with commentary and rabbinic sources please see: Alfred Edersheim, *The Life and Times of Jesus the Messiah*, (Peabody, Massachusetts: Hendrickson Publishers, 1994), 980-1007.

2 Samuel	22:28; 23:1; 23:3; 23:4.
1 Kings	4:33.
1 Chronicles	3:24.
Psalms	2:1; 2:4; 2:6; 2:7; 2:8; 2:9; 16:5; 18:31(32); 18:50; 21:1(2); 21:3(4); 21:5(6); 21:7(8); 22:7(8); 22:15(16); 31:19(20); 36:9; 40:7; 45:2(3); 45:3(4); 45:6(7) 45:7(8); 50:2; 60:7; 61:6(7); 61:8(9); 68:31(32); 72:8; 72:16; 72:17; 80:17; 89:22-25(23-26); 89:27(28); 89:51(52); 90:15; 92:7(8); 92:10(11); 92:12(13); 95:7; 102:16(17); 106:44; 110:1; 110:2; 110:7; 116:9; 116:13; 119:33; 120:7; 121:1; 126:2; 132:18; 133:3; 142:5.
Proverbs	6:22.
Ecclesiastes	1:11; 7:24; 11:8.
Song of Songs	1:8; 1:17; 2:8; 2:9; 2:10; 2:12; 2:13; 3:11; 4:5; 4:16; 5:10; 6:10; 7:6; 7:13; 8:1; 8:2; 8:4; 8:11.
Isaiah	1:25; 1:26; 2:4; 4:2; 4:4; 4:5; 4:6; 6:13; 8:14; 9:6; 9:7; 10:27; 11:1; 11:2; 11:3; 11:4; 11:7; 11:10; 11:11; 11:12; 12:3; 12:5; 14:2; 14:29; 15:2; 16:1; 16:5; 18:5; 21:11; 21:12; 23:8; 23:15; 24:23; 25:8; 25:9; 26:19; 27:10; 28:5; 28:16; 30:5; 30:6; 30:18; 30:19; 30:25; 30:26; 32:14; 32:15; 32:20; 35:1; 35:10; 40:1; 40:2; 40:3; 40:5; 40:10; 41:18; 41:25; 41:27; 42:1; 43:10; 45:22; 49:8; 49:9; 49:10; 49:12: 49:14; 49:21; 49:23; 49:26; 51:12; 51:17; 52:3; 52:7; 52:8; 52:12; 52:13; 53:5; 53:10; 54:2; 54:5; 54:11; 54:13; 55:12; 56:1; 56:7; 57:14; 57:16; 59:15; 59:17: 59:19; 59:20; 60:1; 60:4; 60:7; 60:8; 60:21; 60:22; 61:1; 61:5; 61:9; 61:10; 62:10; 63; 63:2; 63:4; 64:4; 65:17; 65:19; 65:25; 66:7; 68:22.
Jeremiah	3:17; 5:19; 16;13; 16:14; 23:5; 23:6; 23:7; 30:9; 20:21; 31:8; 31:20; 31:31; 31:33; 31:34; 33:13.

Lamentations 1:16; 2:22; 4:22.

Ezekiel 11:9; 16:55; 17:22; 17:23; 25;14; 29:21; 32:14; 36:25; 36:27; 39:2; 47:9; 47:12; 48:19.

Daniel 2:22; 2:35; 7:9; 7:13; 7:27; 8:13; 8:14; 11:24; 12:3; 12:11; 12:12.

Hosea 2:2; 2:13; 2:18; 3:5; 6:2; 13:14; 14:7.

Joel 2:28; 3:18.

Amos 4:7; 5:18; 8:11; 9:11.

Obadiah 18; 21.

Micah 2:13; 4:3; 4:5; 4:8; 5:2; 5:3; 7:6; 7:8.

Nahum 2:1.

Habakkuk 2:3; 3:18.

Zephaniah 3:8; 3:9.

Haggai 2:6.

Zechariah 1:20; 2;10; 3:8; 3:10; 4:7; 4:10; 6:12; 7:13; 8:12; 8:23; 9:1; 9:9; 9:10; 10:4; 11:12; 12:10; 14:2; 14:7; 14:8; 14:9.

Malachi 3:1; 3:4; 3:16; 3:17; 4:1; 4:2; 4:5.

ABOUT THE AUTHOR

Pete Kovacs, B.A., (University of Toronto), B.Ed. (Queen's University), M.Div. (Tyndale University College & Seminary), participated in the Alliance Defense Fund 2002 Blackstone Legal Fellowship as a U.S. constitutional law intern/researcher after his first year of law school, and was a visiting student in Archaeology at the University of Toronto, Near Eastern Studies Department. This is his first book. You can contact the author online and see his current works-in-progress at: www.myspace.com/petekovacs.

www.ingramcontent.com/pod-product-compliance
Lightning Source LLC
LaVergne TN
LVHW011228080426
835509LV00005B/390